Early Intervention and Prevention of Conduct Problems in Children

Stephen Larmar

Early Intervention and Prevention of Conduct Problems in Children

The Implementation and Evaluation of the Early Impact Program for Children and Families At-Risk

LAP LAMBERT Academic Publishing

Impressum/Imprint (nur für Deutschland/ only for Germany)

Bibliografische Information der Deutschen Nationalbibliothek: Die Deutsche Nationalbibliothek verzeichnet diese Publikation in der Deutschen Nationalbibliografie; detaillierte bibliografische Daten sind im Internet über http://dnb.d-nb.de abrufbar.

Alle in diesem Buch genannten Marken und Produktnamen unterliegen warenzeichen-, marken- oder patentrechtlichem Schutz bzw. sind Warenzeichen oder eingetragene Warenzeichen der jeweiligen Inhaber. Die Wiedergabe von Marken, Produktnamen, Gebrauchsnamen, Handelsnamen, Warenbezeichnungen u.s.w. in diesem Werk berechtigt auch ohne besondere Kennzeichnung nicht zu der Annahme, dass solche Namen im Sinne der Warenzeichen- und Markenschutzgesetzgebung als frei zu betrachten wären und daher von jedermann benutzt werden dürften.

Coverbild: www.ingimage.com

Verlag: LAP LAMBERT Academic Publishing GmbH & Co. KG
Dudweiler Landstr. 99, 66123 Saarbrücken, Deutschland
Telefon +49 681 3720-310, Telefax +49 681 3720-3109
Email: info@lap-publishing.com

Herstellung in Deutschland:
Schaltungsdienst Lange o.H.G., Berlin
Books on Demand GmbH, Norderstedt
Reha GmbH, Saarbrücken
Amazon Distribution GmbH, Leipzig
ISBN: 978-3-8433-5394-6

Imprint (only for USA, GB)

Bibliographic information published by the Deutsche Nationalbibliothek: The Deutsche Nationalbibliothek lists this publication in the Deutsche Nationalbibliografie; detailed bibliographic data are available in the Internet at http://dnb.d-nb.de.

Any brand names and product names mentioned in this book are subject to trademark, brand or patent protection and are trademarks or registered trademarks of their respective holders. The use of brand names, product names, common names, trade names, product descriptions etc. even without a particular marking in this works is in no way to be construed to mean that such names may be regarded as unrestricted in respect of trademark and brand protection legislation and could thus be used by anyone.

Cover image: www.ingimage.com

Publisher: LAP LAMBERT Academic Publishing GmbH & Co. KG
Dudweiler Landstr. 99, 66123 Saarbrücken, Germany
Phone +49 681 3720-310, Fax +49 681 3720-3109
Email: info@lap-publishing.com

Printed in the U.S.A.
Printed in the U.K. by (see last page)
ISBN: 978-3-8433-5394-6

THE DEVELOPMENT AND EVALUATION OF AN EARLY INTERVENTION AND PREVENTION PROGRAM FOR CHILDREN AND FAMILIES AT-RISK OF CONDUCT PROBLEMS

Dr Stephen Anthony Larmar

BA   Grad Dip Ed   M Ed   PhD (Psychology)

Abstract

The prevalence of conduct problems in children impacts upon families, educational settings, and broader society within Australia. Conduct problems develop early in an individual's life and can lead to more serious problems including substance abuse and delinquency in adolescence and adulthood. Given the high incidence of conduct problems in children, the need for prevention and early intervention strategies to target the onset and development of this phenomenon is paramount. This book focuses on early intervention strategies for reducing the incidence of conduct problems in children and explores a multi-modal early intervention and prevention program targeting children and families at-risk of the development of conduct problems.

A randomised controlled trial involving 455 children was conducted to evaluate the efficacy of this program. Participants were drawn from ten Education Queensland primary schools in the Mount Gravatt district of Brisbane, Queensland, Australia. The 455 children were randomly assigned to either experimental or control conditions for the purposes of the program's evaluation. From this initial cohort, an indicated sample of 152 participants was identified through a universal screening process. This sample included children who were considered more at-risk of conduct problems. Participants designated to experimental conditions engaged in the school component of the program, with 66 of the experimental group receiving an additional indicated component facilitated in the school setting. Further, a selection of parents of children in the experimental group participated in the home component of the intervention. The retention rate for families engaged in the study was high with 96% of participants remaining engaged in the study throughout the evaluation process.

The findings that emerged from the study revealed significant differences between participants who engaged in the intervention program compared with those designated to control conditions. Positive changes in the behaviour of students reported at the school level were statistically significant. However, while some changes were identified in the home setting, the treatment effects of the program were not significant. These findings were sustained at the six-month follow up period.

Conclusions drawn from this study were conceptualised within the framework of current advances in the social science literature that focus on conduct problems and early intervention and prevention. The outcomes of the research emphasise the significance of comprehensive interventions programs for children and families at-risk that focus on both school and home settings and that are easily implemented in, and cost-effective to, community populations. Recommendations from this research serve to inform future research agendas in early intervention and prevention and specialists in the fields of psychology and education.

Table of Contents

Acknowledgements

I would like to thank Professor Mark Dadds for his dedication, wisdom and support in assisting me throughout the process of conducting the study that ultimately led to the publication of this work.

Thanks also to Professor Ian Shochet for his commitment to providing additional assistance and support during my PhD studies. His personal warmth and insights were appreciated.

To all the participants involved in the study, including teachers, principals, guidance officers, parents and children, thank you for your tremendous assistance in the facilitation of this research.

To Associate Professor Jayne Clapton, Professor Lesley Chenoweth, Dr Jennifer Fraser and Dr Elizabeth Templeton, thank you for your 'listening ears' and timely insights.

My thanks also go to Dr Terence Gatfield, for his friendship and inspiration, both personally and professionally. Thank you for your words of encouragement and ongoing assistance throughout the completion of this work.

Thank you also to Olivia Gatfield for the many hours spent working with participants and helping in the overall facilitation of the project which culminated in the writing of this text. Your assistance has been invaluable.

To Dr Rosemary Lindgren, thank you for your wisdom, love, and generosity.

To Earl, Sue, Margaret, Chris, Rachel, Joel, and Heidi - thank you for your love, friendship and dedication.

Thanks to my dear friends Isaiah, Callan, Michael, Damien, Ulrik, Karen, Kendall, Jenny, Emma, Susanna, Chris, Ruth, Andy, Andrew and Steve for walking the road with me over the last ten years. You are all such a blessing.

Finally, I am enormously indebted to my wife Emma, and children Keelan, Kristian and Tobias for their love and support. Thank you Emma for your wisdom, patience and generosity. I am grateful for all that you have contributed in the process of completing this book. Thank you to the three wise men for all of the fun you share with me and for your fresh perspectives that enrich my life.

Chapter 1: Introduction

The prevalence of conduct problems in child populations is a phenomenon that significantly impacts upon families, educational settings and broader society within Australia (Sanders, Tully, Baade, Lynch, Heywood, Pollard, & Youlden, 1999). Conduct problems include behaviours such as aggression, impulsivity, and delinquency that impede the individual's functioning and cause distress to the individual and significant others. The direct costs associated with the treatment of conduct problems are of growing concern to government departments faced with limited financial and personnel resources. In addition, the long-term benefits of treatments have come into question (Kazdin, 1995). The indirect costs to the community in terms of criminal activity, substance abuse and associated psychosocial problems are substantial (Patterson, DeGarmo, & Knutson, 2000).

While the literature identifies a vast array of existing treatments to address conduct problems in children, the majority of treatments are often administered too late in the child's trajectory towards dysfunction. Most current intervention treatments are designed to reduce the symptoms of conduct problems rather than address influences in the child's world that are associated with the onset of dysfunctional behaviour. In the last decade there has been a shift towards the development of early intervention and prevention frameworks for children and families at-risk (Greenberg, Domitrovich, & Bumbarger, 1999). Such frameworks allow for the early detection and treatment of dysfunction to prevent the individual from moving towards maladjustment.

The literature suggests that early intervention models have potential in the treatment and prevention of conduct problems (August, Realmuto, Hektner, & Bloomquist, 2001; Frick, 1998; The Conduct Problems Prevention Research Group, 2002; Walker, Severson, Feil, Stiller, & Golly, 1998; Webster-Stratton, 1998). Early intervention programs are designed to target individuals identified as at-risk for the development of a disorder. Behaviours identified in such individuals may not be considered clinically significant, however, mild signs of particular problem behaviours may indicate the individual's potential vulnerability to the development of psychopathology.

1

Models of Prevention

Various models have been used to describe types of prevention. One model is based upon the stage in the development of an individual's dysfunction. The first category, primary prevention, refers to interventions that target individuals who have not yet presented signs of a disorder. The focus of primary prevention is on preventing the development of a disorder in the individual. The second category, secondary prevention, refers to those intervention measures targeting individuals who present mild symptoms that do not meet diagnostic criteria for a disorder but indicate the risk of these symptoms developing. These forms of intervention align most closely to the rationale underpinning early intervention models of treatment because the interventions are designed to arrest the further development of presenting symptoms. The final category is tertiary prevention. Tertiary interventions target individuals late in the trajectory of dysfunction at the point in which the individual has been clinically diagnosed. Tertiary interventions serve to alleviate the intensity of the problem by reducing dysfunctional behaviours, thus decreasing the affects of the disorder on the individual and their environment.

Greenberg et al. (1999) outline a second model that also organises preventative interventions into three categories. The first category refers to universal preventative interventions that target a selected population or group. The targeted population is not chosen according to the identification of individuals at-risk within the group. Instead the model is proactive in intent and serves to prevent the development of dysfunction in all participants included in the population. An advantage of universal programs is that they do not require processes of selection to recruit participants therefore reducing the risk of stigmatisation. The cost of such programs, however, can be substantial and the potentially low dosage of treatment offered by such interventions may fail to alter the more at-risk individual's trajectory towards psychopathology (Greenberg, Domitrovich, & Bumbarger, 2001). Further, the facilitation of universal programs requires that considerable attention be directed towards children who are in least need of such interventions, given that the incidence of psychopathology among children is relatively low (Greenberg et al., 2001).

The second category, selective interventions, targets identified individuals or groups of individuals who are at higher risk of developing a particular disorder due to biological or social risk factors. The final category refers to indicated interventions. These interventions target individuals who have not received clinical diagnosis, but are presenting symptoms that indicate a significant risk towards the development of a disorder. Selective and indicated programs can be advantageous in that they are more cost effective and facilitate early identification of target individuals who are in need of such intervention. The major disadvantage of selective and indicative programs is that participants may be at-risk of stigmatisation from their wider peer group as a result of involvement in the intervention (Shochet, Dadds, Holland, Whitefield, Harnett, & Osgarby, 2001).

Early intervention programs may be universally administered, however an emphasis on selected or indicated early intervention models exists in preventative research. Individuals targeted for an early intervention are most commonly identified through a process of screening based on the analysis of presenting symptoms that indicate a propensity towards the development of further dysfunction.

Over the past decade psychologists and educational specialists have given priority to the development of preventative models of treatment. This priority has been significantly influenced by the substantial financial costs incurred through the implementation of expensive intervention treatments that are intended to arrest the affects of conduct problems on society. Further, such interventions are predominantly clinic-based, largely dependent on the referral of the client for treatment and are often administered too late in the cycle of the individual's trajectory towards dysfunction. These forms of intervention are primarily tertiary treatments. That is, they target individuals with diagnosed conditions. Although such forms of intervention are the most common approaches to combating dysfunctional behaviour in children and adolescents, research indicates that preventative models are more effective in addressing conduct problems in at-risk populations (Kazdin, 1995). Preventative treatments are designed to target individuals before they show any significant signs of a disorder. Research indicates that the optimal time to engage at-risk children in the process of treatment is prior to the development of significant symptomology (Greenberg et al., 1999). These findings, in conjunction with recent research results that question the efficacy of some forms of tertiary treatment, have provided impetus for directing future research in prevention (Kazdin, 1995).

Current research in early intervention and prevention lends support to the importance of broader systems in the individual's world that influence the development of conduct problems (Frick, 2000). Where previous treatments have failed to address broader dynamics associated with the individual's dysfunction,

3

current models of treatment emphasise the significance of influences derived from multiple settings in the individual's world. A number of current treatments target risk factors identified in the individual's home and school setting as a means of facilitating more holistic intervention frameworks. Such multicomponent intervention designs have elicited promising results and emphasise the need for further research in prevention that acknowledges dynamics in the home and school settings that influence the onset and development of dysfunction (Cummings, Davies, & Campbell, 2000).

Existing intervention frameworks such as First Step to Success (1998), Fast Track (1999) and Head Start (1998) apply designs that are ecological in breadth to address multiple influences affecting children and families. While these programs differ in content and process, the philosophical underpinnings of each intervention are grounded in theory supporting the influencing factors apparent in the broader ecology of the child's world. The design of these interventions allows for treatment to be administered early in the individual's life as a means of reducing the risk of the development of conduct problems.

In summary, there is a rising concern throughout western society regarding the prevalence of conduct problems in child and adolescent populations. The significant effects of conduct problems on families, educational settings and broader society call for intervention treatments that are preventative in focus in contrast to existing frameworks that aim to reduce the symptoms of conduct problems that have developed late in the trajectory of dysfunction. Current advances in the social science literature also emphasise the significance of multifaceted intervention frameworks that target the broader ecology of the individual including the home and school setting to effectively arrest the onset of conduct problems in community populations.

This book aims to present an evaluation of an early intervention and prevention program for conduct problems in young children. The design of the intervention is informed by existing intervention frameworks that target home and school settings. However, the evaluated intervention extends upon models of treatment by targeting individuals at an earlier age. The majority of existing treatments are administered on a child's entry into primary school. This intervention is designed to target children entering the preschool year. Further, current interventions are overly reliant on trained consultants rendering such programs as financially untenable to the communities they are intended to target. The necessity of trained consultants in the implementation of existing designs also reduces the capacity for such interventions to be easily disseminated in regular community populations.

The evaluated program is titled the Early Impact (EI) program and recognises the influences of interacting systems surrounding the child's world at an individual, home and school level. The home component consists of parent management training that serves to instruct parents in the delivery of strategies and techniques to manage children's behaviours. Further, the training facilitates exploration into some of the key dimensions influencing a child's trajectory towards dysfunction including risk factors present in the familial context. The school component focuses on the teaching of social skills and is universally administered by classroom teachers who are trained in child management techniques consistent with those recommended at the home level. The individual component provides remedial assistance for children identified as 'more at-risk' for ongoing behaviour problems and is facilitated by the classroom teacher or teacher's aide. Comparisons were made throughout the course of the evaluation to determine treatment outcomes using a control/experimental design. An exploration of existing multicomponent models of treatment will be considered in a later section of this book as a means of introducing some of the key characteristics of this form of intervention.

The following chapter defines the term 'conduct problems' and provides background into the prevalence of this phenomenon as drawn from the literature. A review of factors associated with the development of conduct problems in children will also be considered including risk and protective factors. Finally, issues surrounding the treatment of conduct problems will be presented including discussion on the importance of tailoring intervention treatments that consider the individual's broader systems of school and family.

Chapter 2: Conduct Problems in Children: The Current State of the Field

Incidence and Prevalence of Conduct Problems in Children and Adolescents

The effects of conduct problems upon families, schools and other community settings have significant ramifications for society. According to reports issued by the Australian Government Attorney General's Department and the Australian Early Intervention Network for Mental Health of Young People, there is a growing recognition of the need for early intervention frameworks, particularly for preschool aged children (Sanders, Gooley, & Nicholson, 2000; Davis, Martin, Kosky, & O'Hanlon, 2000).

Research focussing on the prevalence of conduct problems in community populations indicates that the rate of children and adolescents exhibiting conduct disorders falls between the range of 2% to 6% (Kazdin, 1995). This range encompasses clinically diagnosable disorders only. The prevalence of conduct problems that present a concern to schools and families and yet fall short of the diagnostic threshold is more difficult to determine.

Referrals to clinic and community services for child and adolescent populations are increasing. According to Kazdin, Siegel, and Bass (1990) between one third and one half of clinic referrals are directly related to conduct problems. The rise in referrals to such agencies has serious implications in terms of the quality and type of service that can be administered given the significant demand for treatment (Greenberg et al., 2000).

There is also concern that conduct problems can be stable and persistent (Kratzer & Hodgins, 1997; Lahey, et al, 1995; Moffitt, 1993; Offord et al., 1992). Recent research by Moffitt (2001) explored the stability of conduct problems over time and identified two distinct pathways. The first pathway, 'life-course persistent' is used to describe the trajectory of a small percentage of individuals who engage in antisocial behaviours at every life stage. The second pathway, 'adolescent limited', delineates those individuals whose antisocial behaviours are temporary and occur during adolescence (Moffitt, 2001). Unlike other forms of antisocial behaviour that would usually correlate with a particular stage of development and diminish during the general course of a child's maturation, life-course persistent conduct problems continue throughout the individual's life beyond childhood and adolescents leading to adult criminality, including violence and drug abuse. Such activity can have serious

6

implications for those individuals, the families and community groups of which they are a part (Moffitt, 2001).

The incidence of conduct problems being passed down intergenerationally is also of concern. The trend towards an individual with conduct problems experiencing conduct problems in their own children is significant. Studies by Brook, Whiteman and Lu Zheng (2002) and Huesmann, Eron, Lefkowitz, and Walder (1984) identify the stability of problem behaviours over time and generations.

The direct cost of conduct problems on society is significant (Greenberg et al., 2000). Children and adolescents who are referred to youth and mental health agencies for conduct problems usually require regular and ongoing intervention treatments given that the course of dysfunction is deeply entrenched. Such interventions draw upon the resources of such agencies at significant cost (Greenberg et al., 2000). The costs incurred in addressing criminal and delinquent behaviours associated with conduct problems are also of concern given the rise in the prevalence of such behaviours in community populations. Personnel involved in the criminal justice system are experiencing the increasing demands associated with combating the effects of juvenile criminal activity on society. Further, the costs of rehabilitation, special education programs and other forms of reactive treatment are substantial for agencies facilitating such services.

Another issue surrounding the prevalence of conduct problems in community populations is the limited capacities of health professionals to engage children and families at-risk in cogent intervention treatments that reduce the impact of this phenomenon on society. Identifying children in need of treatment is often problematic given that they rarely refer themselves for support (Kazdin & Weisz, 1998). While many forms of treatment exist to reduce the affects of conduct problems on families and community populations, many children and adolescents with significant symptomology fail to receive adequate assistance (Knitzer, 1985; Tuma, 1989). Further, the intervention treatments may be administered late in the individual's trajectory towards maladjustment thus rendering such treatments ineffective in facilitating significant change.

In summary, the prevalence of conduct problems is of serious concern and impacts significantly upon health, educational and family systems within the western world. The deleterious affects of conduct problems on children and families are extensive and can continue from one generation to the next. The direct costs to

7

society in terms of criminal activity and mental health services are large and given the incidence of conduct problems in children and adolescents the provision of services to address this phenomenon is inadequate. Further, the efficacy of existing intervention treatments aimed at reducing the impact of conduct problems on society requires further consideration. The following section defines conduct problems as conceptualised within the context of this text. Discussion will also be included to examine the onset of conduct problems and a series of pathways drawn from the literature to delineate an individual's trajectory into dysfunction.

Conduct Problems: Definitions

The term conduct problem refers to those behaviours evidenced in the individual that do not conform to societal norms and encroach on the rights of others (Frick, 2004; Walker et al., 1998). Behaviours may range from mild forms of conflict to significant acts that are in direct violation of the rights of individuals, groups or broader society. Problem behaviours can be evidenced in most children and adolescents during the developmental process. However, there is a strong demarcation between expressions of antisocial behaviour that fall within a normative range for children and adolescents and extreme behaviours that place the individual at-risk of maladjustment. There is an increasing concern surrounding the identification of serious forms of antisocial behaviour for specialists working in the fields of psychology and education. Questions arise regarding the point at which behaviours are considered to move beyond the normative stages of development to behavioural manifestations that are at an appropriate diagnostic threshold (Frick, 1998).

Terms such as conduct disorder (CD) and oppositional defiant disorder (ODD) are used to define the prevalence of clinically significant antisocial behaviours in children and adolescents (McMahon & Wells, 1989). The process of diagnosing children with clinically significant conduct problems involves the identification of a cluster of behaviours that match those identified in the Diagnostic and Statistical Manual of Mental Disorders (DSM-IV-TR; American Psychiatric Association, 2000). The prevalence of formally diagnosed conduct problems in children and adolescents falls between two and six percent of community populations (Kazdin, 1993). These statistics bare substantial consideration given the significant population this disorder affects and the short and long-term ramifications of this phenomenon for society at large.

While the prevalence of clinically diagnosed conduct problems is significant, children and adolescents with sub-clinical levels are also presenting serious concerns to schools, families, and the community. It is important to define conduct problems in broader terms to encompass the population of individuals who do not fall within the clinical range of diagnosis, but whose behaviours place them at-risk for later maladjustment. Children and adolescents with conduct problems often experience multiple problems in adjustment and can be at-risk of engaging in delinquent and criminal behaviours in adulthood (Brook et al., 2002; Frick, 1998; Kazdin, 1995; Vitaro, Brendgen, Pagani, Tremblay, & McDuff, 1999). Discussion regarding the onset of conduct problems in the individual will be examined in the following section.

Onset of Conduct Problems

The literature provides extensive evidence to show that conduct problems develop early in the child's life (Dadds, 1995; Kazdin, 1992; Mc Mahon & Wells, 1989; Walker et al., 1998; Webster-Stratton, 1998). The onset of conduct problems may vary according to the individual, however, there is a propensity for disorders such as ODD and attention deficit hyperactivity disorder (ADHD) to occur in early childhood. CD is often evidenced at a later stage in development. However, research acknowledges the early onset of CD in some children and supports the distinction between the onset of CD in childhood and its manifestation in adolescence (Hinshaw, Lahey, & Hart, 1993; Olson, Bates, Sandy, & Lanthier, 2000; Patterson, DeBaryshe, & Ramsey, 1989).

Child-onset CD classifies those individuals whose dysfunctional behaviours are evident in childhood. The child's symptomology usually consists of behaviours indicative of ODD or ADHD and progress to behaviours that match the diagnostic classification for CD. The disorder is more prevalent in boys, and individuals with child-onset CD are more likely to engage in acts of aggression. Child-onset CD is one of the most serious conduct problems. Recent findings suggest that early onset of conduct problems significantly influences the individual's trajectory into adulthood delinquency (Patterson et al., 2000).

The prevalence of adolescent-onset CD is significantly higher than child-onset CD (Kazdin, 1995). The rates of CD in adolescents are approximately 7% for 12 to

9

16 year olds in comparison to those for children (4% for 4 to 11 year olds). Individuals engaging in criminal behaviours during adolescence, who have not manifested significant conduct problems in childhood are classified within the adolescent-onset category. There is a propensity for a more equal distribution of boys and girls within this sub-type. The influence of the individual's peer group is considered significant in the development of adolescent-onset CD (Laird, Jordan, Dodge, Pettit, & Bates, 2001; McCabe, Hough, Wood, & Yeh, 2001).

The following section provides an examination of key models developed to describe the emergence of psychopathology in the individual including risk factors associated with the onset of conduct problems. Protective factors known to reduce the risk of maladjustment will also be considered.

Pathways to Psychopathology

The literature indicates that multiple pathways to psychopathology exist (Frick, 2004; Frick, 1998; Kazdin, 1994). Contemporary models recognise the mutual interplay of characteristics of the child and his/her surrounding social systems in the development of conduct problems (Henggeler, Schoenwald, Borduin, Rowland, & Cunningham, 1998; Olsen et al., 2000). Dadds views the developmental influences of conduct problems as "... a set of systems, subsystems, and components of systems interacting at the biological, interpersonal, family and social levels" (p. 5, 2002). Frick (1998) also acknowledges the complex interplay of a variety of causal factors in the development of conduct problems including dispositional and environmental influences.

Research has also identified that conduct problems represent a developmental sequence or pathway. Therefore, individuals with conduct problems may manifest changes in behaviour and stability over time as the condition progresses. Different researchers have identified typical pathways to describe the early onset and later development of conduct problems in the individual. The most significant findings follow.

Loeber (1988) identifies two pathways for conduct problems in children. He terms the first the 'aggressive-versatile pathway'. Children showing signs of developing aggressive and covert conduct problems fall into this category. Children within this pathway initially develop aggressive forms of antisocial behaviour. A number of these individuals move on to offences that are exclusively violent, while others, as a result of influences in an earlier stage of life, engage in both aggressive and non-aggressive acts. Individuals in this latter group may become involved in the destruction of property as well as violent delinquent acts.

The second pathway is defined as the 'non-aggressive antisocial pathway'. This pathway describes the development of non-aggressive, covert acts in children. Individuals in this category engage in non-aggressive antisocial behaviours in childhood that develop into non-aggressive behaviours in adulthood such as theft and destruction of property.

Research by Loeber, Wung, Keenan, Giroux, Stouthamer-Loeber, Van Kammen, and Maughan (1993) identified a similar model of causality for psychopathology in child populations. Three pathways to delineate the development of conduct problems in children were identified. The first pathway is identified as the 'authority-conflict pathway' where the child initially presents stubborn behaviours that progress to acts of defiance and finally to authority avoidance behaviours. The 'covert behaviour pathway' primarily describes the escalation of covert behaviours. The child initially engages in minor covert behaviours such as lying or shoplifting, progresses to behaviours involving damage to property and finally commits serious acts of delinquency including breaking and entering and car theft. The final pathway, the 'overt behaviour pathway', describes the development of aggressive behaviours. This pathway identifies behaviours such as bullying and annoying others as evidence of the first step in the development of overt behaviours. The child progresses to behaviours including physical fighting as a next step. Finally, acts of extreme violence can emerge.

As mentioned in an earlier section of this book, Moffitt (2001) also delineates two pathways of antisocial behaviour. The 'life-course persistent' pathway describes a smaller group of individuals who engage in antisocial behaviour throughout their lifetime. Such individuals manifest antisocial behaviours as they develop from childhood into full maturation. As new social situations arise in the course of the individual's development, different problem behaviours emerge. Moffitt (1993) argues that the nexus of 'life-course persistent' antisocial behaviour lies in the interaction between the individual's neuropsychological vulnerabilities and criminogenic environments. The 'adolescent limited' pathway encompasses a larger group of persons who partake in delinquent behaviours for a temporal period (Moffitt, 2001). The etiology of adolescent limited antisocial behaviour consists of a gap between biological and social maturity, involves the individual modelling learned antisocial responses from others and is sustained through reinforcement.

The preceding models focus on dynamics in childhood and adolescents that influence the development of problem behaviours later in life. The following model by Olsen et al. (2000) focuses more specifically on infant populations and is used to delineate specific risk factors influencing the trajectory of problem behaviour into middle childhood.

Olsen et al's. (2000) model accounts for the development of serious forms of maladaptive behaviours that can be identified in infant and pre-school-aged children and emphasises that these behaviours can persist in the transition to middle childhood. The model suggests that early child behavioural and care giving risk factors are linked to the emergence of conduct problems in the developing child. Verification of the model indicated the link between the quality of the caregiver's relationship to the at-risk child and the development of conduct problems in later childhood. The model also describes a distinct correlation between the child's 'difficultness' and resistance to control and later onset of conduct problems. While these models assist in explaining the development of psychopathology in children, research has identified specific variables placing children at-risk of developing conduct problems (Frick, 2004; Kazdin, 1993; Rutter, 1989). The following section examines risk factors that are commonly applied to children and families at-risk of conduct problems.

Risk Factors

The examination of various risk factors and their interplay with the individual's ecology provide significant insights into the dynamics associated with the onset of dysfunction. Such factors have been explored extensively in the literature to determine the significance of their interaction with the individual. Many risk factors have been identified and can be categorised within the broader domains of characteristics associated with the child, parent and family and educational setting.

Child Characteristics

The child's temperament, which comprises those characteristics of personality influenced by genetic constitution and environmental factors during pregnancy and birth, is another factor that may increase the likelihood of the child developing conduct problems (Caspi, Henry, McGee, Moffitt, & Silva, 1995; Caspi & Silva,

1995; Dodge & Pettit, 2003; Frick, 1998; Frick & Morris, 2004; Henry, Caspi, Moffitt, & Silva, 1996; Loeber & Farrington, 2000; Moffitt, 1993; Moffitt & Caspi, 2001; Raine, 2002). Children who exhibit behaviours reflective of a 'difficult' temperament are known to be at-risk for the development of problems later in life (Rutter, 1989). The mutual interplay between the child's temperament and parental control in early childhood may also serve to increase the risks of later dysfunction (Bates, Pettit, Dodge, & Ridge, 1998; Olsen et al., 2000).

Callous-unemotional (CU) traits evidenced in the individual with conduct problems also serve to increase the risk of the development of later dysfunction. In a study by Frick, Cornell, Barry, Bodin and Dane (2003) examining the influence of CU traits on future maladjustment, it was found that children with problem behaviour who also exhibited CU traits had a tendency to display thrill and adventure seeking behaviours. Further, children with CU traits were less sensitive to the cues of punishment when reward-oriented approaches were encouraged and less responsive to threat or emotional distress in comparison to other children with conduct problems (Frick et al., 2003). Findings of this investigation identify how the influence of CU traits may serve to delineate specific developmental pathways to severe antisocial behaviour.

Moffitt and Caspi (2001) identify the personal and genetic dimensions influencing the child's susceptibility to the development of psychopathology. Genetic disposition is a component known to influence the development of severe conduct problems and later delinquency (Rutter, 1989). Studies investigating the role of genetic factors in the development of maladjustment have provided evidence of the biological influences contributing to the emergence of conduct problems in children (Caspi, McClay, Moffitt, & Mill, 2002; Jaffee, Caspi, Moffitt, Polo-Thomas, Price, & Taylor, 2004; Moffit & Caspi, 2001; Reitsma-Street, Offord, & Finch, 1985). Recent findings recognise the interactivity of genetic factors associated with the individual and their surrounding environment. Research by Caspi et al. (2002) exploring childhood maltreatment as a universal risk factor for problem behaviour, recognises the influences of genotype on the development of later dysfunction. Inferences drawn from recent investigation into the influences of genetic factors on the development of conduct problems provide initial evidence to suggest that the gene encoding the neurotransmitter-metabolizing enzyme monoamine oxidase A (MAOA) serves to moderate the effects of maltreatment on the development of dysfunctional behaviour

13

in males (Caspi et al., 2002). Jaffee et al. (2004) also recognise the genetic factors that influence antisocial behaviour and that mediate the child's experience of corporal punishment. Their research acknowledges that genetic factors that influence harsh discipline in adults are largely the same as those that influence problem behaviour in children.

Familial Characteristics

Another significant factor contributing to the emergence and maintenance of behavioural disorders in children is the influence of family. Prior investigations acknowledge interpersonal dynamics within the family as a major contributing factor to the development of conduct problems (Henry et al., 1996; Hollenstein, Granic, Stoolmiller, & Snyder, 2004; Kazdin, 1995; Loeber, Drinkwater, Yin, & Anderson, 2000; Loeber, Farrington, Stouthhamer-Loeber, Moffitt, Caspi, & Lynam, 2001; Loeber, Green, Lahey, Frick, & Mc Burnett, 2000). Criminal behaviour and other forms of psychopathology evidenced in the parents such as depression and substance abuse place the child at-risk for further dysfunction (Reid, Eddy, Fetrow, & Stoolmiller, 1999). Aversive parenting practices such as aggressive or extreme punitive measures or inconsistent forms of discipline are also commonly identified in parents whose children exhibit conduct problems (Bor & Sanders, 2004; Henry et al., 1996; Jaffee, Caspi, Moffitt, & Taylor, 2004; Kazdin, 1995; Loeber et al., 2001; Silburn et al., 1996). Dysfunctional interactions between the parent and child including lack of parental acceptance and limited displays of warmth and affection resulting in less attachment are also consistently demonstrated characteristics in the families of children at-risk of psychopathology (Coie et al, 1993; Kazdin, 1993; Loeber, Farrington, Stouthhamer-Loeber, & Van Kammen, 1998; Shaw, Winslow, Owens, & Vondra, 1998). The level of parental involvement in the child's activities and quality of parent supervision are also determinates in the development of conduct problems in children. Further, marital disharmony is another factor that may increase the risk of conduct problems developing in the child (Frick & Loney, 2002; Henry et al., 1996).

Research has identified low socio-economic status as another contributing factor to the onset of externalising disorders in children (Coie et al., 1993; Keiley, Bates, Dodge, & Pettit, 2000; Loeber et al., 2001; Webster-Stratton & Hammond, 1998). Poverty and its associated effects on the family can significantly influence the

14

development of conduct problems in the child (Frick, 2004; Kazdin 1995). Other factors influenced by low socio-economic status may also elicit familial dynamics contributing to the development of psychopathology. These factors include poor child supervision due to limited financial resources (e.g., parents working while the child is at home) and increased parental stress as a product of the pressures faced in providing for the family (Kazdin, 1995; Loeber et al., 2001).

School Environmental Characteristics

Another risk factor supported by the literature includes characteristics of the school environment (Frick, 2004; Kazdin, 1995). Such characteristics may include factors such as organisation, socio-demographic characteristics, class size and other dimensions of school culture. In a seminal study by Rutter, Maughan, Mortimore, and Ouston (1979) a number of school settings were examined to determine particular factors influencing behavioural outcomes in children. The study identified specific characteristics that appeared to reduce the incidence of maladaptive behaviours in student populations. These characteristics included an emphasis on academic tasks, the teacher's planning, formulation and implementation of experiences of learning, teacher encouragement, an emphasis on students exercising responsibility, physical working conditions conducive to student learning, teacher availability to address student problems, and clear and consistent teacher expectations. The measurement of these variables across a range of settings gave support to those school characteristics that serve to decrease the risk for conduct problems.

Peer rejection and the child's alliance with deviant peer groups in the school setting can also contribute to the development of dysfunction (Dishion, Nelson, Winter, & Bullock, 2004; Snyder, Prichard, Schrepferman, Patrick, & Stoolmiller, 2004; Vitaro et al., 1999). Individuals with conduct problems often experience rejection from regular peer groups (Frick, 2004; Laird et al., 2001; Frick, 1998). This rejection process serves to deny the child opportunity to learn pro-social behaviours from supportive peer relationships. Such experiences of social isolation may also influence the child to associate with antisocial peer groups. Children and adolescents with conduct problems often identify with peers who engage in antisocial or deviant behaviour (Laird et al., 2001; Vitaro et al., 1999). Longitudinal studies have also indicated that individuals who exhibit aggressive and impulsive behaviours and have poor peer relationships are at-risk of adult criminality, substance abuse and

15

psychiatric disorders (Loeber et al., 2001; Rutter, 1989). Through the individual's involvement with antisocial peer groups, deviant behaviours are reinforced and exposure to pro-social ways of functioning is diminished.

This section examined a number of risk factors associated with the development of conduct problems in children and adolescents. The identification of variables associated with the individual's heredity, familial influences and school environment were examined to determine their influence on the development of psychopathology. The following section delineates a number of protective factors consistent in the research literature and examines the impact of such factors on the course of dysfunction.

Protective Factors

The literature has identified a range of protective factors that reduce the risk of individuals developing conduct problems. Protective factors serve to ameliorate those risk factors present in the individual's life promoting resilience. Greenberg et al. (1999) outline three categories of protective factors including:

1. personal attributes of the individual including cognitive ability, social competence and the individual's temperament;

2. the individual's interaction within their immediate and broader environment. Such interactions include a secure attachment to parents as well as other individuals who provide emotional and/or psychological support and who demonstrate pro-social values; and

3. the interacting systems in the individual's world such as school and home relations, the quality of the educational system with which the individual is a part and regulatory activities.

Coie et al. (1993) delineate four ways that protective factors may influence the individual. The first is to directly decrease dysfunction. The second is to counteract risk factors reducing their affects. The third is to interrupt the cycle from risk to maladaptive outcome. The final means by which protective factors operate is to prevent the risk factors from taking hold in the individual's life.

While research into protective factors influencing the course of deleterious outcomes is still relatively recent, further investigation into protective factors is necessary in order to provide individuals and families with the most cogent forms of intervention treatments for conduct problems. Future advances in prevention must

16

consider the means by which protective factors can be developed in the individual to reduce the risk of psychopathology.

This section has considered a number of risk factors associated with the development of conduct problems in the individual as well as protective factors that serve to reduce the risk of maladjustment. The following section considers issues associated with the treatment of problem behaviour in children and adolescents.

Issues Surrounding Treatment of Conduct Problems

An understanding of the risk factors affecting those individuals who present with conduct problems is imperative to the tailoring of intervention treatments that combat maladaptive outcomes. An overarching concern for researchers in prevention and specialists working in community health and education is that many of the individuals and families most in need of intervention programs are failing to access available treatments (Greenberg et al., 2001; Spoth, Goldberg, & Redmond, 1999). This trend is largely influenced by the families' isolation from such treatment programs due to personal characteristics and socio-environmental factors (Biglan & Metzler, in press; Spoth, Redmond, Hochaday, & Yeol Shin, 1996). The need for screening individuals and families at-risk has emerged given the failure of such groups to access intervention treatments provided for the community. Further, the high attrition rate for families accessing mental health services due to barriers in the intervention process significantly affects treatment outcomes (Kazdin, Holland, & Crowley, 1997; Kazdin, 1996; Kazdin, Prinz, & Miller, 1994). Current research in prevention recognises the importance of tailoring intervention programs to the needs of the client groups for which such programs are intended to increase client engagement (August, Egan, Realmuto, & Hektner, 2003). The following section examines a range of existing models of treatment for children with conduct problems.

Common Treatments for Early Intervention and Prevention of Conduct Problems

Numerous studies have explored clinic, school and family-based interventions to arrest the development of conduct problems (Dupper & Krishef, 1993; Hartman, Stage, & Webster-Stratton, 2003; Kastner, 1998; Kazdin, Ayers, Bass, & Rodgers, 1990; Kendall, 1993; Patterson, DeGarmo, & Forgatch, 2004; Sanders, 1999; The Conduct Problems Prevention Research Group, 2002; Webster-Stratton, Reid, &

17

Baydar, 2004). This section examines the most recent forms of treatment to combat conduct problems in children and adolescent populations.

Treatment models that include family interventions such as parent training and individual or group social cognitive modalities have been shown to produce significant results (Dadds, 2002; Kazdin, Siegel, & Bass, 1992; Webster-Stratton et al., 2004;). Family interventions include approaches such as parent training where parents are taught skills to alter their child's behaviour. These approaches also target maladaptive familial interactions that may serve to sustain anti-social responses in the home setting (Kazdin, 1993; Patterson et al., 2004). Studies by Prinz and Miller (1996) and Sanders (1999) support the efficacy of family interventions in the short and long term.

Social-cognitive treatments combine cognitive and behavioural techniques to teach problem solving skills. These can include strategies such as modelling, role-play, feedback and reinforcement. Various investigations evaluating the effectiveness of social-cognitive treatments have indicated the benefits of such forms of intervention in arresting the development of conduct problems in children (Frick, 1998; Lochman & Wells, 1996; McMahon & Wells, 1989; Walker et al., 1998; Webster-Stratton, Reid, & Hammond, 2001).

Specialist personnel working in the domains of psychology and education have also focussed on preventative measures in an attempt to address and reduce the impact of conduct problems in child and adolescent populations upon educational contexts (Dishion, McCord, & Poulin, 1999; Kastner, 1998; Kazdin & Kagan, 1994; Kendall & Panichelli-Mindel, 1995; Little & Hudson, 1998; McCord, Tremblay, Vitaro, & Desmarais-Gervais, 1994). Children and adolescents exhibiting conduct problems are often enrolled in schools where traditional approaches to teaching and learning fail to accommodate the type and frequency of problems encountered (Hoff & DuPaul, 1998; Soodak & Podell, 1994). As a result teachers and other school personnel are often faced with significant challenges in the management of students with conduct problems. To alleviate the stresses associated with the affects of problem behaviour on the regular classroom, teachers, administrators, and educational specialists have developed and implemented school-based interventions to provide ongoing support to this population of students (Hovland, Smaby, & Maddux, 1996).

While the various treatments cited above may produce clinically significant results, the point at which the parent, child or adolescent engages in treatment can

18

markedly influence treatment impact (Dadds, 1995; Kazdin, 1993; Walker et al., 1998). As indicated, a growing concern regarding intervention models of treatment for children and adolescents with conduct problems is that treatments are often administered too late in the cycle of the child's trajectory towards dysfunction (Walker et al., 1998). Children and adolescents are referred for treatment during the course of development when manifested behaviours may have already become entrenched.

There is also a concern with the emphasis on intervention treatments that are applied within the framework of a single treatment modality. These approaches confine such treatments to a single context that fails to address critical factors in alternative settings influencing the individual's dysfunction (Henggeler et al., 1998). Issues such as low parental and teacher participation may arise through the employment of treatments that are limited in focus and fail to consider broader variables attributing to the development of psychopathology in the child.

In the last ten years there has been a rise in interest in intervention programs for children and families at-risk of conduct problems that are ecological in breadth. The literature emphasises the multidetermined nature of conduct problems and the importance of tailoring intervention programs that target risk factors in the individual's psychosocial environment (Frick, 2004; Frick, 1998; Greenberg et al., 2001). A number of current programs have been evaluated to determine their effectiveness in preventing the onset of problem behaviour. These programs target children early in the trajectory of dysfunction and are designed to impact upon dynamics in the home and school setting that are placing the child at-risk of maladjustment. The following section provides a review of existing intervention frameworks that target multiple settings as a means of reducing the risk of psychopathology in children and families as an introduction to the study outlined in this book.

Early Intervention and Prevention Programs for Children and Families At-Risk of Conduct Problems

In the previous section of this book discussion centred upon specific risk factors associated with the development of conduct problems in children and adolescent populations. A number of protective factors that serve to reduce the risk of the development of dysfunction were also examined. Later discussion focussed on issues surrounding the treatment of conduct problems in child and adolescent populations. The following section examines the efficacy of a number of current models of early intervention including discussion on the impact of such models on a population of at-risk individuals to identify areas for future research in prevention.

Current Treatments
Prevention and Early Intervention Models of Treatment

Studies by Webster-Stratton (1998), Walker et al. (1998) and the Conduct Problems Prevention Research Group (2002) support the effective influences of early intervention models on child and adolescent problem behaviour. A summary of these models and findings corresponding to the effectiveness of such interventions follows.

Webster-Stratton (1998) examined the effectiveness of a selected intervention program designed to arrest the onset of conduct problems for preschool age children. The program targets parents whose strategies of management place their children at-risk and focuses on assisting parents to replace maladaptive parenting strategies with more effective ones. Family characteristics that place children at-risk for developing conduct problems including low socio-economic status, high levels of stress, single parenthood, marital discord, and depression were identified. Parenting behaviours such as inconsistent discipline and physical abuse were also acknowledged as factors contributing to the onset of conduct problems. Webster-Stratton's research focussed on children in the Head Start population, a preschool organisation targeting socio-economically disadvantaged families. Children from the Head Start program were targeted for inclusion based on their exposure to a higher level of risk factors associated with the development of conduct problems.

The program was evaluated by randomly assigning children enrolled in Head Start centres to either experimental or control conditions. Children and parents in the experimental group engaged in the Partners intervention developed by Carolyn Webster-Stratton. The Partners intervention "...is guided by developmental theory concerning the role of multiple risk factors (aspects of the child, family, and school) in the development of conduct problems" (Webster-Stratton, 1998, p. 718). Prior investigations examining Partner's effectiveness with clinically referred children indicated its potential in arresting the development of conduct problems in children enrolled in Head Start programs.

The parents of participants in the experimental group were trained in specific child management practices taken from a theory-based parent training program. The parent training was delivered by trained family service workers and focussed on strengthening the competence of parents and encouraging parent involvement in the child's schooling. Teachers of child participants also underwent training to familiarise themselves with the parenting strategies of management advocated by parent trainers. The teachers were encouraged to employ similar strategies within the classroom context to create consistency across the home and preschool setting. Teacher training also involved a focus on supporting parent involvement in the children's schooling. This combination served to facilitate a selective intervention. The control group engaged in standardised curriculum administered as part of the Head Start organisation.

Initial recruitment of participants for the study involved accessing parental consent, providing parents with information explaining the nature of the intervention and targeting specific Head Start family service workers and teachers for inclusion in the study. Prior to the implementation of the intervention participants in the experiment and control group were subjected to identical baseline assessments consisting of home observations, parent interviews, and teacher and parent questionnaires.

Parenting measures for screening and the evaluation of outcomes consisted of questionnaires, completion of standardised and adapted instruments and independent observations in the home setting. Parent participants completed questionnaires during structured interviews with trained clinical staff. Questionnaires assessed participants' parenting skills, approaches to discipline, and the level of support for the child's education and social development. Parents completed selected measures including those assessing demographic and family risk factors.

Independent observations were carried out in each participant's home. Six trained observers familiar with the selected observation measures completed the observations. Observations were conducted for approximately 30 minutes and involved observing mothers interacting with their child in the home setting. Observers were not informed of those participants who were subjected to the experiment or control conditions. Teacher measures were completed to assess the frequency and severity of the child's dysfunction in the school setting and the level of parental involvement in the child's learning and development.

The intervention lasted for eight to nine weeks. Throughout the duration of the intervention, participants were closely monitored using trained observers. Standardised materials were included across the intervention sites and comprehensive, quality training was offered to assure treatment integrity.

Results at post-test obtained through the same measures employed during the pre-intervention phase and through teacher questionnaires focussing on student performance identified significant improvement in the behaviour of the intervention group compared with the control. Follow-up assessments revealed that differences were maintained in parent discipline practices and teacher reports of child behaviour at 12 and 18 months following participation in the intervention. Webster-Stratton's research into the efficacy of the Head Start intervention revealed its positive impact on children at-risk for the development of conduct problems.

The First Step to Success program (Walker et al., 1998) is another model of intervention that has proven to elicit promising results indicating its potential effectiveness in arresting the development of problem behaviour in at-risk populations. First Step to Success is a selected intervention program targeting kindergarten-age children at-risk of developing conduct problems. The program was evaluated to determine its effectiveness as an early intervention model. It was formulated in response to the increasing number of children enrolling in schools who were identified with early signs of antisocial behaviour. The program consists of three components: universal screening and early detection; school intervention; and home based parent training. The program focuses on teaching children pro-social behaviours to assist in the promotion of academic and social success.

In an investigation by Walker et al. (1998) two cohorts of at-risk kindergarten children engaged in the First Step to Success program. The first cohort, consisting of 24 children, completed the program in 1993 and 1994. The remaining cohort of 22 children completed the program over the following two years. The study's design consisted of a randomised, experimental, wait-list control group design to evaluate the intervention's effectiveness. Children were screened for participation in the program using the Early Screening Project (ESP) procedure (Walker et al., 1994). This procedure involves a series of four stages and "...integrates teacher rankings, teacher ratings, and in vivo behavioural observations across the sequential screening stages" (Walker et al., 1998, p. 69). The ESP is designed for children enrolled in preschool

22

and kindergarten settings and has indicated discriminative validity in the educational and psychological literature.

During stage one of the screening all kindergarten teachers in a selected district were invited to participate in the study. A presentation was organised to communicate the key tenets of the program and the nature of the teacher's involvement in it. The teachers who chose to participate were asked to identify five children in their kindergarten group whose behaviours closely matched a list of standardised behaviours for externalising disorders. The same teachers were to choose another five students whose behaviours closely aligned with a standardised description of internalising behaviours. According to the descriptors corresponding to either externalising or internalising behaviour the teachers ranked the children from the most evident characteristic to the least. The three highest-ranking students in stage one were included for screening in stage two.

Stage two of the screening involved the completion of selected behavioural measures by the classroom teacher. These measures provided further insights into the nature and severity of the child's behaviour based upon comparisons of normative levels for the age of the target group.

Children were selected for stage three if the resulting scores exceeded normative levels for the ESP. This stage involved direct baseline observations of the target students in the kindergarten setting by trained observers including project coordinators and other personnel involved in the program's implementation. Observations centred upon the target student's engagement in academic tasks and social responses during times of teacher instruction (Academic Engaged Time; AET). Students selected for the third stage of screening "...whose baseline levels of AET averaged 65% or lower and/or who scored one or more standard deviations above the Child Behavior Checklist Aggression subscale's normative mean, were selected for possible inclusion in the study" (Walker et al., 1998, p. 70). Parents of these students were contacted to provide explanation of the nature and intention of the intervention and to seek parental consent for the child's inclusion. The intervention was implemented over a period of approximately three months. Eight program consultants were trained to assist in the implementation process and were allocated two to three cases each throughout the implementation phase.

Targeted children and their parents were involved in the home and school components. The home component involved training the parents in specific strategies to build child competencies in areas that affect school adjustment. These strategies include skills such as positive communication and sharing, cooperation, limit setting and friendship making. The home component includes weekly lessons and activities taught to the parent by the program consultants in the parent's home. The parent is encouraged to employ the acquired skills in their interaction with the child and to form a partnership with the child's teacher to strengthen the links between home and school.

The school component consists of the target child's engagement in an adaptation of the CLASS program (Hops & Walker, 1988) designed for use with conduct disordered primary and elementary grade students. The CLASS program involves the use of a home and school reward system that monitors the frequency of the child's pro-social behaviours. The administering of rewards is contingent on the child demonstrating a series of positive behaviours over a designated time period. Towards the conclusion of the program the class teacher phases out the rewards.

The CLASS program is run over a thirty-day period and involves three phases. During each day of the program either the consultant or teacher, dependent on the program phase, facilitates a 20 to 30 minute session with the student. Each session focuses on the completion of activities exploring the benefits of positive behavioural choices.

In the first phase (consultant phase) of the program the consultant describes the program to the teacher, parent, child and their peer group and assumes responsibility for the program's implementation over the first five days. The consultant works collaboratively with the teacher and parent to tailor the school based component to most effectively address the needs of the target child. In the second phase (teacher phase) the teacher facilitates the program over a period of fifteen days. During this time the teacher implements the daily program and communicates with parents to provide feedback regarding the student's progress. The final phase (maintenance phase) involves a reduction of the external rewards utilised in earlier phases of the program and an increased emphasis on praise and encouragement from the teacher and parent. This phase is designed to decrease the child's dependence on the program strategies to encourage greater internal motivation to choose adaptive behaviours.

During the investigation a series of methods were included to monitor treatment integrity. Consultants and teachers were required to keep daily records to track their use of the reward system. Consultants also kept written logs describing their perceptions of critical events that occurred during the intervention. These perceptions were discussed at regular intervals with the program coordinators. The school and home base components were structured in a way that facilitated standardised delivery. The home base component did not include a system for recording the parent's deployment of the strategies recommended.

The program was evaluated using a randomised experimental design. Five dependent measures were used to examine participants' performance in the intervention. Three of the measures used in the ESP were included at post-intervention including the Teacher Ratings of Adaptive Behavior, Teacher Ratings of Maladaptive Behavior, and AET observations. The targeted children's teacher completed the first two measures. The trained observers who recorded the pre-intervention AET observations completed the third measure. The final two measures included the Aggression and Withdrawn subscales. Post-intervention data analysis revealed a significant increase in pro-social behaviours in the intervention group in contrast to the control group at post-intervention. These results were sustained at one-year follow-up.

A comparative early intervention model, the Fast Track program developed by the Conduct Problems Prevention Research Group (2002), is presently being trialed to determine its effectiveness among a population of at-risk students. Fast Track is an early intervention program developed to assist in the promotion of competencies for those children identified as at-risk for the development of conduct problems. The program combines universal, selective and indicated models of prevention and is longitudinal in design. The intervention involves the family, school, peer group and community in an attempt to target multiple risk and protective factors. The program is designed to target children at the point of school entry and addresses aspects of the child's environment that may lead to school failure. The components of the intervention are developed to target factors in the child, the family, and the classroom hypothesised to be a significant risk to the child's development.

The child component consists of universal classroom instruction through the delivery of an adapted version of the PATHS curriculum. The curriculum is taught throughout the first grade with an average of two to three lessons being conducted each week. Program coordinators assist in training teachers in the delivery of the PATHS curriculum and provide ongoing consultative support to monitor the fidelity of implementation. The curriculum covers four specific skills including emotional

25

understanding and communication, friendship, self-control and social problem solving.

The child component is selective in that it provides group social skills training and academic tutoring for approximately two-hours each week over a seven-month period during the first year of implementation for all target students. In addition, target students engage in peer support sessions involving classroom peers and trained tutors to promote pro-social skills instrumental to the development of friendship formation. These tutors also provide academic tutoring sessions during school hours two to three times each week.

The parent component of the program includes organised training sessions focussing on parenting strategies to assist the child in their adjustment to school and to encourage positive behaviours. The concepts explored in the parent training include establishing the development of a positive partnership between home and school, encouraging parent self-control, establishing age appropriate expectations for the child's behaviour and the development of parenting skills to facilitate a positive relational dynamic between the parent and child. Training techniques employed in the parent component include facilitator instruction, modelling, role-play and group discussion.

In addition to parent training, the parent component also includes home visits during the weeks between training sessions. This provides program consultants with the opportunity to support staff in the home to facilitate parental empowerment and self-efficacy (Conduct Problems Research Prevention Group, 1999).

A trial of the Fast Track program was implemented across four sites with schools organised into two sets matched on demographic variables and randomly assigned to intervention and control conditions. Kindergarten age children at-risk for the development of conduct problems were identified through a multi-stage screening system involving both teacher and parent ratings of disruptive behaviour. Teachers in the 54 participating kindergartens rated the behaviours of all children using the Authority Acceptance Scale of the Teacher Observation of Classroom Adaptation (10 items).

Parents of those children identified in the top 40% of the sample were contacted and requested to complete a 24-item measure. Items were developed from the aggression scales of the Child Behavior Checklist and additional contributions of the researchers. These measures were used to ascertain the frequency and severity of problem behaviours identified in the home. The teacher and parent rating scores were averaged to identify those students in the top 10% considered at high risk. These students were invited to participate in the study with the mean age of participants being 6.5 years.

The experimental group consisted of 445 children in 191 classrooms and the control group included 446 children across 210 classrooms. The target students were identified for inclusion in the intervention at the conclusion of the kindergarten year. Parents of the target children were briefed on the organisation and philosophy underpinning the program and were invited to participate.

Methods to facilitate treatment integrity were employed throughout the intervention process. Intervention consultants and principal investigators conducted regular observations of all intervention staff and feedback was given regarding the delivery of skills involved in the implementation of the program.

Parent and teacher data were collected either at the child's entry into year one and/or immediately following the target child's first year of school. Rating forms were completed in the home and school by parents and teachers respectively. Behavioural observations were also conducted across home and school. Trained observers unaware of participant treatment conditions completed observations at home and school based on four separate sessions.

Twelve measures were employed to assess the child's aggressive-oppositional behaviours. A selection of these were utilised for the purposes of screening while others served to evaluate treatment outcomes to determine improvements in the child's behaviour during the first year of the intervention. Referral to school records to acquire information regarding the use of special-education services in grade one was included as well as measures assessing child behaviours during home observations.

Measures were also employed to determine the targeted children's social-cognitive skills. Student achievements based on test scores and related school records were also assessed at the end of year one to determine the child's reading capacity and school performance. Child social competency was rated through parent's completion of the Social Competence Scale in combination with a peer nominations procedure identifying those students who were perceived by their peers to be cooperative members of the class. Peer ratings were collected from children in the participating classrooms following parental consent. These ratings were used to ascertain those

27

students who were 'most liked' and 'least liked' according to related behavioural descriptors. A series of parent measures were also included: the Parent Questionnaire; the Parent-Teacher Involvement Questionnaire-Parent; The Developmental History interview; and the Ratings of Parent Change. These measures provided information on parenting practices, the family's history over a twelve-month period and the extent of change in parent's practices over the initial twelve-month period of the intervention.

Evaluation analyses completed at the 3-year period of the intervention trial revealed that children assigned to treatment conditions were less likely to exhibit serious problem behaviours compared to children designated to control conditions. The children in the intervention group displayed significant improvements in terms of the acquisition of skills considered to be critical protective factors to arrest the development of anti-social behaviour. Parents in the intervention group also demonstrated significant improvements in terms of their parenting practices and school involvement compared with those in the control group.

The Fast Track program is a long-term intervention designed to continue through the middle school years. Post intervention data of a longitudinal nature cannot yet be evaluated to draw conclusions relating to the program's longer-term effects. The intervention is continuing with the original cohort identified for inclusion in the study and is in its fifth year.

This section has examined three exemplary current early intervention models cited in the literature and reported on the initial impact of each on a selected population of children. Methods and procedures utilised in each intervention were delineated as a means of identifying key attributes of each model that proved effective in reducing the incidence of conduct problems in young children. While these intervention treatments have shown promising results, further research is required to fully develop and evaluate community-based programs for the early identification and prevention of conduct problems. The next section describes an alternative early intervention model formulated by the author designed to address limitations evident in existing models of prevention and assist in directing future research in the prevention of conduct problems through the model's evaluation.

Limitations Identified by the Literature Review

While prior investigations of early intervention have identified some positive effects in the short-term, further research is required to evaluate the effectiveness of alternative early intervention models of treatment for infant age (pre-school to year two) children encompassing the home and school (Greenberg et al., 1999). The early onset of conduct problems in infant-aged children necessitates the development of models of intervention that facilitate earlier screening in order to engage the at-risk child at the point in which their symptoms first become apparent. Further, an intervention framework that broadens the ecological emphasis of current approaches through an increased focus on the school teacher's engagement with the at-risk child would serve to provide greater ecological breadth to current intervention measures. The study described in this book examined the potential effectiveness of an early intervention program based on a broader ecological approach to arrest the development of conduct problems in young children as a means of contributing to the current body of knowledge focussed on early intervention models of treatment.

Existing models of early intervention focus on the screening of children prior to year one and expose the child to treatment conditions on their entry into elementary school. This process precludes those pre-school age children in need of early intervention at the point of pre-school entry.

There is also a need for an intervention design that delineates a clear framework for the child's teacher in addressing antisocial student responses in the classroom and broader school setting. Previous models have employed trained consultants as part of the school based component to assist teachers at the classroom level. This approach relies significantly on the consultant's expertise and may impede the teacher's utilisation of their own skills to effectively manage the class group. Further, these models have provided limited support to the classroom teacher particularly in the development of explicitly defined strategies of management that would enhance the broader intervention process.

The costs incurred through the implementation of existing models of treatment, both financially and in terms of the personnel needed to direct these interventions, are also substantial. Future models need to be more cost effective in design to address the implications of exorbitant costs associated with the delivery of existing early intervention models of treatment.

Summary and Conclusions

An investigation of existing intervention frameworks designed to arrest the development of conduct problems in children has indicated the significance of formulating modes of treatment that encompass the child's broader environment including home and school settings. A number of existing models have proved efficacious in the treatment of children at-risk of conduct problems. However, multimodal intervention programs targeting children and families at-risk of conduct problems have not yet been tested in Australia. Further, evidence has emerged from the research reviewed that indicates the need for the development of alternative intervention frameworks that build upon existing treatments.

The aim of the Early Impact Program evaluation, therefore, was to evaluate the effectiveness of an early intervention and prevention program for children and families at-risk of conduct problems. Further, the study attempted to evaluate factors necessary for the successful implementation of an intervention that address the limitations identified in existing models of treatment. The hypothesis that an early intervention and prevention program for children and families at-risk that centres upon the psychosocial dynamics of home and school would reduce the incidence of conduct problems was tested. The effectiveness of this intervention would be evidenced by: a) reduction in the incidence of acting out behaviours in both the home and school setting as observed by parents and teachers respectively; b) reduction in teacher and parent stress associated with the management of child behaviour; c) increased skill for parents and teachers in effectively managing child behaviour; and d) evidence of improved behaviours exhibited by children engaged in the program at the end of the intervention period and at six-month follow-up. Further, the hypothesis that the aforementioned intervention treatment would have high social validity in regular community populations was also considered and measured in terms of participant engagement and satisfaction with the intervention design and the implementation process.

The intervention evaluated is titled the Early Impact (EI) program. This program was developed by the author and is similar in design to existing intervention treatments in that it encompasses variables within the home, school and community. Given the literature's strong indication that conduct problems are multiply determined, consideration was given to the development of a comprehensive model of

30

treatment that targets multiple risk factors associated with the development of psychopathology.

EI consists of two overarching components, the school component and the familial component and is divided into two intervention phases, the intensive phase and the extended phase. The two components are designed as complimentary components and each includes strategies designed to encourage adaptive adjustment in the target child. The delivery of selected strategies also serves to facilitate consistency across the home and school contexts. The intensive phase of EI is implemented over a period of ten weeks with an extended phase providing 'booster treatments' for the remainder of the school year. It is intended that the intensive phase be implemented in the second term of the academic school year.

As part of the school component, teachers involved in the intervention process are trained in specific strategies of management by qualified trainers working in the domains of psychology and education. Training equips teachers and related school personnel to implement a school behaviour management framework and complimentary curriculum developed by the author.

An overarching intention of the EI program is that the curriculum and strategies of management be implemented in preschool to year two classes. The intervention is designed to 'catch' this population of students. Kazdin (1995) suggests that early intervention models of treatment must target children at the point at which the intervention will have the most significant impact. Research suggests that early intervention programs are most efficacious for at-risk students with an age range between four to seven years (Kazdin, 1995).

Whereas the school component of EI combines a universal and selective approach, the home component of the EI program is selective in focus. Parents of children identified as at-risk are invited to participate in an intensive parent training program that forms part of the broader intervention. The parent training is conducted over six sessions and is based on an existing parent training model developed by scholars in the field of child psychology. Individuals involved in the facilitation of the sessions undergo training in the implementation and delivery of the parent training component. A more comprehensive description of the EI program is presented in a later section of this book.

An investigation examining the effectiveness of an early intervention program focussed on psychosocial variables within the home, school and broader community was conducted to assist in filling the research gap. The evaluation of the EI program served to examine the potential effectiveness of this model of intervention to provide a broader framework for understanding the dynamics associated with the prevention of conduct problems in young children.

According to Webster-Stratton (1998) the efficacy of early intervention programs that address conduct problems in children at a broader level including an emphasis on dynamics within the home, school and broader environment requires further investigation. Webster-Stratton's research suggests that future studies should be conducted to explore the effectiveness of early intervention and prevention treatments that facilitate stronger partnerships between families, schools and the broader community in addressing the development of conduct problems in children.

Research Focus

The specific aims of the study were to assess:

1. The social validity of the EI program for regular school community groups and for children and families at-risk of conduct problems.
2. The effectiveness of the EI program for children and families identified as at-risk for conduct problems.

In accordance with these aims, the following hypotheses and questions were tested.

The first hypothesis to be tested was that the EI program would demonstrate high social validity as demonstrated by: (a) high participation rates; (b) high retention rates; and (c) high satisfaction rates.

The second hypothesis to be tested was that the EI program would be associated with reductions in the incidence of problem behaviour in children. From this hypothesis, five research questions were developed:

First, would the school component of the EI program reduce the incidence of problem behaviour in children in the school setting? Second, would the school component encourage greater pro-social responses in children in the school context? Third, would there be a decrease in parents' use of aversive parenting strategies as a result of parents engaging in the EI program? Fourth, would the home component of the program serve to reduce problem behaviours in children in the home setting? Finally, would there be an increase in pro-social behaviours in children in the home setting as a result of the home component of the EI program?

The intention of the evaluation was to make an original contribution to the academic literature in addition to providing a more informed platform for practitioners in psychology and education. Research into the effects of early intervention programs designed to arrest the development of conduct problems in children is instrumental in assisting psychologists and educators to develop more effective interventions for child populations. Findings of such exploration serve to assist practitioners and families in becoming better informed regarding the critical psychological variables related to behaviour change. In addition, resulting programs may aid practitioners through the provision of alternative therapeutic approaches. Further, such research would provide an outline for the development of effective early intervention treatments within a broader psychosocial framework.

This chapter has provided an overview of existing models of early intervention and prevention designed to arrest the development of conduct problems in children. The models identified emphasise the significance of the child's ecology in the development of psychopathology and focus on reducing risk factors prevalent in multiple settings in the child's world. An initial description of the EI program was also provided including key components of the intervention that build upon existing models of treatment. Further, a series of hypotheses and related research question were presented that served to guide the investigation. The following chapter describes the methodology adopted for the study.

Chapter 3: Introduction to the Early Impact Program Evaluation

The theoretical framework underpinning the EI study which has been considered in an earlier section of this book, focussed on an ecological model of psychopathology for children at-risk of the development of conduct problems. This ecological framework provided insight into the nexus of psychopathology in children, describing the various risk factors associated with this population and thus informed the design of the intervention and its evaluation. This broad ecological model of psychopathology provided a theoretical foundation for the aims and intentions of the intervention, as well as its structure and organisation. Further, the model also informed the outcomes to be measured as part of the intervention's evaluation.

Participants

The initial cohort of students included as part of the evaluation to test the hypotheses outlined in this text consisted of 455 children with an age range of four to five years. The participants were drawn from ten Education Queensland primary schools in the urban district of Mount Gravatt, Brisbane, Queensland. This district was selected on the basis of its existing cohort of schools whose current enrolments included a significant population of students (approximately 3% to 5%) with conduct problems. School recruitment for the study involved approaching the ten principals of the identified schools to participate in the research following official approval from Education Queensland's Mt Gravatt District Office for the research to be carried out. Schools were matched in pairs on the basis of socio-economic status and size and then, within each pair, randomly assigned to be either an experimental or control group.

The 455 children were enrolled in the preschools of the ten schools participating in the study. This initial sample size facilitated universal screening of participants to identify those at-risk of developing conduct problems. The identified sample following screening comprised 135 children. Of these 135 children, 5 moved to alternative schools during the course of treatment, leaving a remaining cohort of 130 participants. Sixty-six of the participants were enrolled in one of the five schools that engaged in the intervention program. The remaining participants (69) were drawn from the five remaining schools and were designated to control conditions to assess changes in baseline behaviours.

Given the number of participants included in the study, the power of the statistical analysis was adequate (i.e. 0.8) to measure a moderate effect size using an alpha level of 0.05. Cohen (1992) recommends that to achieve power of 0.8 at a significant testing level of $p<0.05$, n=60 are required to detect moderate effect sizes and n=24 are required for a large effect size. Previous research has indicated medium to large effect sizes are typically achieved in such interventions. The sample size was also considered by drawing upon the example of a number of prior investigations focussing on problem behaviour and treatment effects. Studies by Gresham, Lane, MacMillan and Bocian (1999), Shaw, Winslow, Owens and Vondra (1998), Shaw, Owens, Vondra, Keenan and Winslow (1996), Shelton, Barkley, Crosswait, Moorehouse, Fletcher, Barrett, Jenkins and Metevia (2000), and Walker et al., (1998), were examined and a sample size of approximately 120 participants was calculated based on the average sample size (n=121) of the previously identified investigations.

Participant Screening

Screening of participants for inclusion in the study was conducted in the first term of the academic year. This provided the time necessary for identification of participants for inclusion in the study and allowed for the implementation of the intervention in the following school term. Screening involved two stages.

Screening Stage One

In the first stage of screening, the cohort of preschool teachers in the participating schools nominated students in their respective classes who they considered to be at-risk for the development of problem behaviour. This initial nomination process involved teachers using a class list and a standardised description outlining characteristics commonly associated with a child with externalising behaviours (see Appendix A). The standardised description was developed by the author and comprised an adaptation of descriptors for externalising behaviours derived from the DSM-IV (APA, 1994) and Child Behavior Checklist (CBCL) (Achenbach & Edelbrock, 1991). The class list included each child's name and an accompanying one-item likert scale corresponding to each child. The scale enabled the teachers to indicate whether each child was: often like the child described; sometimes like the child described or; rarely like the child described in the

35

standardised description. Those children who the teacher perceived to be 'often or sometimes like the child' described were included for the second stage of screening.

Screening Stage Two

In the second stage of the screening process a confirmation checklist corresponding to each nominated child was used to determine participant suitability for inclusion in the investigation (see Appendix B). The checklist included the suitability criteria identified below, as well as a section enabling teachers to comment on other variables commonly associated with children at-risk. These variables included symptoms of problematic anxiety, language delays and other learning problems. Children who met the corresponding suitability criteria for the study were included as the final sample. Participant suitability criteria included: age (four to six years); teacher nominations derived from the screening process; parental consent for involvement in the study; no other identifiable major mental or physical illness including neurological impairment; and absence of Attention Deficit Hyperactivity Disorder, except those participants whose ADHD problems were controlled by prescribed medical treatment but who continued to present with significant externalising behaviours. Of the final cohort included in the investigation there was a relatively balanced gender distribution between the experimental and control groups.

Utility of the Screening Procedure

Prior to screening, consent forms were sent to all parents of children enrolled in the ten schools participating in the trial (see Appendix C). Of the entire cohort (635), 509 parents consented to their children's participation in the study. Self-report questionnaires were administered to all parents (509) who had consented to their child's participation in the research. 455 (89.78%) questionnaires were completed at pre-intervention. Sociodemographic information gathered from the completion of the 455 respondents is presented in Table 1. Response numbers varied given that some respondents failed to complete certain questions.

Recruitment Procedure

At the commencement of the academic year, parents of all children included in the preschool cohort of the participating schools were sent a letter of consent detailing the nature and intention of the investigation as well as the extent of the child's participation in the research. Parents were requested to read the letter and return the accompanying consent form indicating their willingness to consent to the child's participation in the study. Following the first and second stages of screening, all parents of children in the intervention group were contacted by letter and invited to attend a series of child management training sessions.

Evaluation Measures

Family Domain

All parents of children participating in the study were invited to complete baseline self-report measures focused on their perceptions of the child's behaviour and their child management practices. These measures were distributed through each preschool's internal mail system in the eighth-week of the first term of the school year (baseline) and at post-intervention and six month follow-up. Accompanying the measures was a letter providing explanation of how the measures were to be completed as well as the dates when they were to be returned to the preschool (see Appendix D). All teachers were also familiarised with the procedures involved in completing the measures to offer additional assistance where necessary. In addition, the author's contact details were outlined in the letter with an invitation for parents to contact the author at any time if they required additional assistance.

37

Table 1

Sociodemographic Profile of Respondents to the Participation Questionnaire

Characteristics	n	%
Gender (Male)	244	53.6
Gender (Female)	211	46.4
Age		
4 years	303	66.5
5 years	152	33.5
Number of Siblings		
<1	48	10.5
1-2	366	80
3-4	39	8.5
5	2	1
Age of mother		
19-24	15	4.3
25-30	47	13.7
31-40	244	70.8
41-60	39	11.2
Age of father		
21-25	4	1.3
26-30	23	7.5
31-40	213	68.7
41-63	70	22.5
Sole parent	38	8.5
Two parent family	393	87.7
Step Family	17	3.8
Family income		
<$5000	3	.7
$5000-$12000	6	1.4
$12001-$20000	27	6.5
$20001-$30000	46	10.9
$30001-$40000	43	10.2
$40001-$50000	58	13.9
>$50000	230	55.5
Educational Level (mother)		
12 years or more	380	84.6
10 years or less	57	12.6
7 years or less	9	2
No schooling	3	.7
Educational Level (father)		
12 years or more	377	90.7
10 years or less	29	6.9
7 years or less	9	2.2
No schooling	1	.2
Speaks English as a second language	30	6.7

Child Behaviour. Parents completed the Strengths and Difficulties Questionnaire (SDQ; Goodman, 1999) (see Appendix E). The SDQ was developed for the purpose of identifying behavioural and emotional problems in children and adolescents. This measure consists of 25 items and produces scores on five subscales including: conduct problems; hyperactivity; emotional symptoms; peer problems; and pro-social behaviour. For the purposes of this study, the SDQ served to assess parents' perceptions regarding the extent to which each child exhibited externalising and/or internalising behaviours. Parents responded to a 3-point likert scale to rate the existence or frequency of oppositional, defiant and internalising behaviours. In a recent Australian study that assessed the psychometric properties of the SDQ with a large community sample (Hawes & Dadds, 2004), the instrument demonstrated moderate to strong internal reliability and stability on all subscales. Adequate validity was also shown in terms of the relationship of all scales to one another. Further, the pattern of correlations between the SDQ subscales, teacher-ratings and diagnostic interviews demonstrated sound external validity.

Family Function. Parents completed an adaptation of the Alabama Parenting Questionnaire (APQ; Shelton, Frick, & Wooton, 1996) (see Appendix F). The APQ consists of several subscales that identify both positive and negative parenting styles that correlate with the development of conduct problems in children. The author revised questions drawn from the parenting supervision subscale of the APQ to more accurately reflect parenting practices and child behaviours for preschool aged children. This adapted measure consisted of 41 items and assesses parenting function, including levels of engagement between the parent and child and general parenting practices. Questions focus on areas including the parent's approach to discipline, their perceived interaction with the child, and their level of interest in the child's world. Parents were invited to respond to each item using a 5-point likert scale. In an Australian study focussing on the evaluation of the APQ, results demonstrated good internal consistency, validity, and test-retest reliability for the measure when tested on a large community sample of four- to nine-year-old Australian children (Dadds, Maujean, & Fraser, 2003).

Diagnostic Interviews. In addition to the evaluation measures stated above, DSM-IV diagnostic interviews were conducted at six-month follow-up using the

Diagnostic Interview Schedule for Children, Adolescents and Parents (DISCAP) (Holland & Dadds, 1995). Parents of those children identified as at-risk, as well as parents of a random selection of non-at-risk children were interviewed. Trained clinical psychologists facilitated the interview process. The diagnostic interviews served to identify those individuals who met sub-clinical and full clinical diagnoses at post-intervention. Completion of the DISCAP facilitates DSM-IV diagnoses and categorises the severity of each diagnosis according to a rating scale from 1 to 6. Reliability checks were included as part of the interview process. A second interviewer (listener) engaged in 20% of the interviews. A reliability standard of no less than 80 percent was met for each diagnostic interview. Results were accepted as statistically significant at the $p<0.01$ level. Correlations obtained from the diagnostic interview scores for the highest rate of severity on the independent assessments were significant at the level of .97. This correlation indicated adequate reliability on levels of diagnosis. An Australian study by Johnson, Barrett, Dadds, Fox, and Shortt (1999) examined the psychometric properties of the DISCAP for DSM-IV disorders in children and adolescents. Interrater agreements on primary diagnoses were high, and rating scale data supported the concurrent and discriminant validity of the DISCAP diagnoses.

School Domain

A series of measures were employed at the school level to determine changes in baseline behaviours of children participating in the study and to assess each child's engagement with the broader class group. Measures were completed in the sixth week of first term (baseline) and at post-intervention and six month follow-up.

Child Behaviour. All teachers in the experimental and control groups completed the teachers' version of the Strengths and Difficulties Questionnaire (SDQ – Teacher; Goodman, 1999) (see Appendix G) for a selection of students in their respective classes. Like the SDQ parent measure, the SDQ (Teacher) consists of 25 items and produces scores on five subscales including: conduct problems; hyperactivity; emotional symptoms; peer problems; and pro-social behaviour. SDQ (Teacher) has moderate to strong internal reliability and stability on all subscales. Adequate validity is also shown in terms of the relationship of all scales to one another. The SDQ (Teacher) also demonstrates sound external validity (Hawes & Dadds, 2004).

40

Teachers were informed by the author that they were to complete the measure for a randomly selected sample of students in the class group. All at-risk students identified in the screening process were included in the final sample. For each class group, the sample consisted of ten students, approximately five who were identified as at-risk for ongoing behaviour problems, as well as another five students who represented a normative sample of children in that age group. This randomised selection process was designed to reduce the potentially stigmatising affects resulting from informing teachers as to the identity of those at-risk students identified during the screening process. The author visited each teacher of the participating preschool cohort during the three stages of data collection, provided explanation of how the measure was to be competed, and collected the completed measures for each school.

General Classroom Behaviour. School observations were also conducted in the fifth week of term one (baseline) and at post-intervention and six month follow-up to assess the general behaviour of the class group. All teachers completed the Classroom Observation Schedule (Larmar & Dadds, 2002) (see Appendix H) over a one-week period. Observations focussed on the general classroom behaviours of students during each session of the school day (morning session, middle session and afternoon session). At the conclusion of each session teachers completed the Classroom Observation Schedule. The schedule consists of a 6-item likert scale identifying the frequency and type of a number of standardised externalising behaviours exhibited by any individual in the class group. The checklist also includes a general class rating enabling the teacher to record their general perceptions concerning the behaviour of the group, as well as a rating to describe the teacher's perceived level of confidence in managing the class. These ratings served to determine any changes in the group's behaviour and changes in the teacher's confidence in managing the class group during the course of the intervention period. An independent observer (preschool teacher aide) also engaged in the observation process using the same observation checklist to ensure inter-observer reliability. At six-month follow-up three trainee teachers received one day of training in order to serve as independent observers, blind to the study's conditions. They completed 20% of the classroom observations to ensure inter-observer reliability. Of the 20% (n=42) of independent observations, there was no less than 80 percent agreement between the teachers and independent observers throughout each day of the observation process.

41

Correlations between scores obtained from the teachers and trainee teachers from the classroom observations were taken at six-month follow-up and calculated for each variable on the Classroom Observation Measure. Correlations were considered significant at the .01 level. The correlation on each variable were: (a) .74 (off task behaviour); (b) .88 (disrespectfulness); (c) .50 (failure to follow directions); (d) .61 (physical and verbal aggression); and (e) .68 (group behaviour). In general, these correlations indicate adequate reliability on the variables of the classroom observation measure.

Peer Perceptions. Peer ratings were completed in the sixth and seventh week of first term (baseline) and also at post-intervention and six month follow-up. Following parental consent, children in each participating class group were interviewed by the author using the Peer Nomination Interview Schedule (Larmar & Dadds, 2002) (see Appendix I). The Peer Nomination Interview Schedule is a 12-item measure adapted from a 17-item peer nomination instrument developed by Crick and Grotpeter (1995). The measure includes six subscales that assess pro-social behaviour, overt aggression, relational aggression, isolation, peer acceptance and peer rejection.

Treatment Integrity and Process Measures of Treatment Implementation and Engagement

Several measures were developed for the purposes of this study to determine implementation fidelity for teachers, parents and the behaviour consultant involved in the intervention process. A description of these measures follows.

Teacher Measures

To measure teacher consistency in implementing the strategies and curriculum developed for inclusion in the program all teachers involved in the intervention completed the Teacher Self Report (TSR) (Larmar & Dadds, 2002) (see Appendix J). The TSR is a 15-item questionnaire that measures the teacher's level of engagement in the program and their consistency in facilitating the program curriculum. The TSR also measures the teacher's satisfaction with the program design. Questions focus on the teacher's consistency in applying classroom management strategies, delivering the program curriculum to the class group and the degree to which regular contact is maintained with students' parents. The TSR also measures the teacher's capacity to encourage full student participation, including the provision of remedial assistance to those students in need of additional teacher support. In addition, the TSR provides information concerning the teacher's perceived levels of stress in managing the class group and confidence in delivering the program curriculum. The TSR was administered at pre-, post and six-month follow-up throughout the evaluation process. At the same designated periods when the TSR was completed, the author met with all teachers involved in the program to assess their progress in implementing the curriculum and strategies. The meeting consisted of a semi-structured interview based on the teacher's responses to the TSR in order to acquire further information relating to the teacher's perceptions of their experiences in delivering the program.

Parent Measures

To ascertain parent levels of engagement in the home component of the program, parents of children in the intervention group completed the Parent Self Report (PSR) (Larmar & Dadds, 2002) (see Appendix K) at the conclusion of the intensive phase of the intervention and at six-month follow up. The PSR includes five items identifying parents' general perceptions of the recommended strategies included as part of the home component of the program design. Items measure parents' consistency in applying the recommended parenting strategies, confidence in using the strategies in the home context and regularity with which parents maintain contact with the child's teacher. Parent trainers also recorded parenting levels of attendance in the training component of the program.

Behaviour Consultant Measure

At post-intervention a behaviour consultant employed by Education Queensland and included as part of the intervention process completed the Behaviour Consultant Report Form (BCRF) (Larmar & Dadds, 2002) (see Appendix L). The BCRF is a 7-item measure that ascertains the behaviour consultant's level of engagement with those children identified as at-risk. In addition, the measure identifies the degree to which the consultant utilised remedial strategies that closely aligned with the intervention's goals and related curriculum.

43

Evaluation Procedure

Outcome Measures

Following parental consent for children to participate in the study, baseline data were collected in week five of the school year. Baseline measures were distributed to all parents of participating children through each of the preschool's internal mail systems with an accompanying cover letter explaining the process involved in completing each measure. A contact phone number was also included as part of the cover letter with an invitation for parents to contact the author if they required assistance in completing the measures. The author met with teachers of each preschool cohort and each teacher completed the various instruments in the school setting. In addition, the author conducted interviews with each participating child as a means of completing the peer nomination schedule. Post intervention and 6 month follow-up data were completed using the same procedures as those during the collection of baseline data. Diagnostic interviews were also conducted at 6-month follow-up for those children identified as at-risk as well as a selection of children representing a normative sample. The interviews were facilitated to determine what children met sub-clinical and full clinical diagnoses at post-intervention. Parents were interviewed by clinical psychologists with reliability checks administered for 20% of the interviews to maintain an acceptable standard of interrater agreement. A reliability standard of at least 80% was met for each diagnostic interview. Table 2 presents a schedule delineating times in which outcome measures were completed throughout the course of the evaluation. Outcome measures considered for inclusion in the study were selected according to their reliability and validity to evaluate the intervention program.

Treatment Integrity and Process Measures

To measure teacher, parent and the behaviour consultant's levels of engagement in the intervention program a series of treatment integrity and process measures were designed for the purposes of the study. Each measure recorded the regularity with which teachers, parents and the behaviour consultant employed the recommended strategies developed within the program's framework. Measures also recorded teacher, parent and the behaviour consultant's perceived levels of confidence in delivering suggested strategies as well as their satisfaction with the program's organisation and the training component of the program. In order to develop reliable measures consistent with the organisation of the intervention, the author referred to measures employed in similar studies to ensure their internal consistency. Table 3 provides an overview of the schedule outlining the administration of each measure.

The EI Program Intervention

Of the ten schools included in the evaluation, five of the schools' preschool cohort participated in the EI program. The three components of the program: the universal school component consisting of teacher training in specific strategies of management and a social skills curriculum designed for implementation in the classroom; the universal home component including parent training in child management practices that can be employed in the home setting; and the indicated component offering one-on-one support by a trained behaviour support specialist for children exhibiting greater risk of developing problem behaviour were facilitated throughout the evaluation. The author, in collaboration with a program assistant, provided training and support throughout the evaluation process. The training and consultative support served to assist teachers, school administrators and parents in the implementation and facilitation of the various components of the program. The following section provides an overview of the implementation of the three components of the intervention.

Table 2

Summary of Outcome Measures (baseline, post-intervention and 6 months follow-up)

Domain	Measured Outcome	When Measured	How Measured	How Administered	Comment
Child behaviour (home environment)	Parent perception of child's behaviour	Term one (baseline), term two (post-intervention), 6 month follow-up	Strength and Difficulties Questionnaire	25 item self-report	Psychometric properties established
Child behaviour (home environment)	Clinical significance of conduct problems	6 month follow-up	Diagnostic Interview Schedule for Children, Adolescents and Parents	Diagnostic interview facilitated by a trained clinician	Psychometric properties established
Child behaviour (school environment)	Teacher perception of child behaviour	Term one (baseline), term two (post-intervention), 6 month follow-up	Strengths and Difficulties Questionnaire – Teacher Version	25 item self-report	Psychometric properties established
Parent function	Levels of attachment and parent child management practices	Term one (baseline), term two (post-intervention), 6 month follow-up	Alabama Parenting Questionnaire	41 item self-report	Psychometric properties established
Peer acceptance (classroom environment)	Peer perceptions of child	Term one (baseline), term two (post-intervention), 6 month follow-up	Peer Nomination Schedule	12 item interview schedule administered by author	Psychometric properties established

Table 3

Summary of Treatment Integrity and Process Measures (baseline, post-intervention and 6 months follow-up)

Domain	Measured Outcome	When Measured	How Measured	How Administered	Comment
Teacher engagement in intervention	Teacher delivery of program curriculum and strategies of management	Term two (post intervention), 6 month follow-up	Teacher Self-Report	15 item self-report and interview	Internal consistency
Teacher satisfaction with program design	Teacher perceptions of quality of program	Term two (post intervention), 6 month follow-up	Teacher Self-Report	15 item self-report	Internal consistency
Parent engagement in intervention	Parent delivery of child management strategies	Term two (post intervention)	Parent Self-Report	5 item self-report	Internal consistency
Behaviour consultant service delivery	Behaviour consultant consistency in providing remedial support	Term two (post intervention), 6 month follow-up	Behaviour Consultant Self-report	7 item self-report	Internal consistency

47

School Component

The implementation of the school component of EI included teacher training in the implementation of specific strategies of management that could be universally applied to each class group. The strategies are delineated in the EI teacher's manual, *Encouraging Positive Behaviour in the Classroom* (Larmar, 2002). These strategies are underpinned by sound educational theory and encourage a framework of classroom management that is democratically focussed and that acknowledges the needs of both students and the classroom teacher. As part of the program implementation process, classroom teachers involved in the research attended a one-day training workshop to receive instruction in the facilitation of the program. The first focus of training explored various strategies of management that form a general framework for the teacher's management of a class group and, more specifically, children with challenging behaviours. The second focus examined the EI curriculum and provided instruction in the facilitation of the curriculum in a regular classroom setting. All sixteen teachers and teacher-aides involved in the study attended one day of training in the EI intervention implementation process.

Strategies of Management. The strategies of management recommended as part of the school component of EI are underpinned by sound educational theory and have been drawn from a broad selection of classroom management frameworks identified in the educational literature. The strategies are best facilitated in a classroom that is democratically centred. As part of the teacher-training program, teachers were encouraged to examine their own approaches to classroom discipline. A number of management styles were explored including laissez-faire, democratic and autocratic approaches. The democratic approach to discipline was recommended as the most congruent to the underlying philosophy of the EI program.

Recommended strategies identified within the program's framework include: setting of limits and boundaries; facilitating a classroom environment where both the teachers' and students' needs are acknowledged; establishing an inclusive and learning enhancing physical classroom space; positive teacher communication; strategies to redirect inappropriate behaviour; the use of logical consequences including timeout; the facilitation of class meetings; and strategies to encourage

48

cooperative partnerships between teachers and parents in order to strengthen the link between home and school.

The EI Curriculum. Teachers and teacher aides in the experimental group were trained in the EI curriculum. An outline of the EI curriculum is provided in the EI program manual, *The Early Impact Program: A Program for Encouraging Positive Behaviour in Young Children* (Larmar, 2002). Curriculum formulated for the intensive phase of the program was explored with the trainer providing specific instruction to assist participants in implementing the curriculum throughout the ten-week duration of the intensive phase. Curriculum designed for the extended phase of the intervention was considered as part of the training to assist in the facilitation of the curriculum over the remaining six months of the school year. The curriculum formulated for the extended phase of the intervention is designed to consolidate student learning experienced during the intensive phase of the program. A number of teaching strategies were also introduced as part of the training process to assist participants in administering the curriculum during the two to three half-hour sessions per week during the intensive phase. Teaching strategies centred upon the concepts explored in the curriculum including: positive communication; friendship formation; social problem solving; developing self-control; and engaging in pro-social behaviours. As part of the training participants were familiarised with the extended phase of the program including the organisation and content of a series of half hour booster sessions that are designed for implementation on a weekly basis for the remainder of the school year. Participants were also familiarised with related student activities that are experiential in focus and designed to reinforce the concepts communicated throughout the curriculum. All school personnel involved in the training process were reminded of the significance of the teacher's direction in the implementation and facilitation of the curriculum. Attention was directed towards the curriculum design and its organisation into discrete modules, providing simple lesson plans for ease of interpretation and integration into the class' existing curriculum. It was also stressed throughout the training process that the curriculum is intended to provide a flexible framework for the teacher, with suggested experiences of learning formulated to accommodate a range of teaching and communication styles and to ensure teachers are not enslaved to the program.

Behaviour Consultant Remedial Assistance. In addition to teacher training in classroom management practices and the program curriculum, a behaviour consultant was trained in the implementation of the indicated component of the program. During the course of the intervention's implementation, classroom teachers were given instruction to assist them in identifying those students regularly exhibiting externalising behaviours. A simple identification checklist was given to the teacher to assist them in ascertaining those students who required additional assistance during the course of the intervention. As part of this process emphasis was given to the teacher's observation of the type and frequency of behaviours identified in specific students to ascertain whether such students could be classified as at-risk for ongoing dysfunction. Following this identification process the teacher referred the student to a behaviour support specialist employed by Education Queensland who worked in collaboration with the teacher to provide additional support. The specialist attended the teacher training workshop to familiarise themselves with the program curriculum as a means of facilitating support that was congruent to the program's goals and philosophy. They also worked in collaboration with the author to ensure that the remedial support provided throughout the program evaluation aligned with the integrity of the program. It was intended that the regularity with which the specialist met with the student be contingent on the severity of the student's behaviour as well as the availability of the specialist to provide additional support. The behaviour support specialist worked for approximately one half hour session each week with the identified students throughout the intensive phase of the program.

Home Component

The home component of the EI program consists of training parents in specific child management practices that can be implemented in the home setting. Key strategies and associated information about positive parenting practices are presented in the EI parent's manual, *Encouraging Positive Behaviour in Young Children* (Larmar, 2002). These strategies and ideas are based on current advances in the psychological literature and are underpinned by sound principles drawn from the fields of early childhood and psychology. Parents of children participating in the program were encouraged to attend a series of parent training sessions focussed on constructive approaches to managing young children. The training was facilitated over three 120-minute training sessions. However, this framework can be adapted to

50

facilitate the parent training process over six 60–minute sessions. Parent trainers included in the study received approximately two days of training in the EI Parent Training Program. The five trainers held post-graduate qualifications in either education or psychology and had extensive experience in working with children and families at-risk. In addition, three of the five trainers were accredited instructors of alternative parenting programs. Each session of the parent training program was designed to encourage participant interaction and trainers working collaboratively with the parent participants to explore the content presented in the program manuals. The parent training framework focuses on behavioural principles of child management and emphasises key factors associated with proactive parenting. The content presented throughout the parent training program includes: a parent's values, beliefs and experiences and the ways these factors influence the parenting role; parental authority; child development and influences underlying a child's behaviour; positive communication; rule and limit setting; parent consistency; strategies to reinforce appropriate behaviour; consequences and timeout; problem solving and problem ownership; exercising assertiveness; managing anger; quality time; and parent preservation. The strategies presented in the training sessions closely aligned with key strategies included in the school component that encourage teachers to employ similar strategies in the classroom setting. This served to facilitate consistency for the child across the home and school contexts. Throughout the training sessions program facilitators strongly encouraged parents to take an active interest in the child's schooling to facilitate closer links between parents and teachers. A summary of the program framework is presented in diagrammatic form in Figure 1.

Children in the control schools were subjected to usual care. Teachers of this group were instructed to manage their respective classes using those behaviour management strategies they felt most comfortable with. In addition, teachers were also encouraged to deliver the regular school curriculum and engage in associated teaching practices aligning with the school's overarching curriculum and management framework. Any children in this group who were identified as at greater-risk during the course of the intervention were referred to the Mt Gravatt district's Behaviour Support Service as a means of accessing additional support. Referral to this agency is the usual process for children at-risk. All referred children were entered into the Behaviour Support Service's database and placed on a wait list in order of priority. Those children who did access specialist support during the course of the investigation were excluded from the final cohort so as not to compromise the study's findings.

Figure 1. EI Program Framework

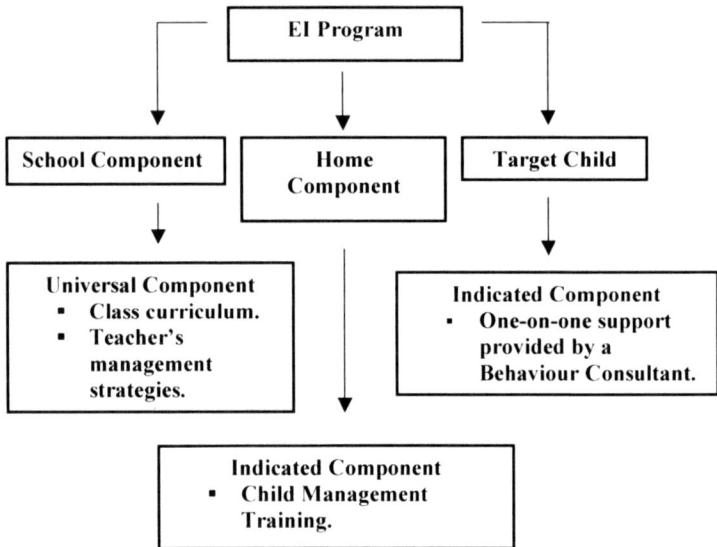

This chapter has provided a description of the general method of the study as well as a detailed description of the program under evaluation. The following chapter presents the results of the EI evaluation including treatment effects within the home and school domain.

Chapter 4: Results of the Early Impact Program Evaluation

As mentioned in the previous chapter of this book, participants involved in this study were grouped according to the school in which they were enrolled and randomly assigned to either experimental or control conditions according to schools. To ensure that the groups were the same at pre-intervention, students in the intervention group were compared with those in the wait-list control cohort on demographic, child behaviour at the home and school level, and parenting strategies of management. ANOVA (SPSS) was used to test the significance of differences between means at pre-intervention. Results at the .05 level of probability were accepted as statistically significant and are shown in Table 4. No statistically significant differences were found on any variables of the EI group compared with those of the control cohort. By the 6-month follow-up period 16 children had withdrawn from participation in the trial: 2 children (1%) from the EI group and 14 (6%) from the control group. The reason for the withdrawal of the children was that parents decided to relocate their child to an alternative school during the course of the academic year. There was no evidence to indicate that the children who withdrew from the study were significantly different from the cohort who remained engaged in the evaluation.

Table 4.

Summary of Baseline Characteristics

	Experimental (n=212)		Control (n=243)	
	M	SD	M	SD
Mean age of children in years	4.37	.49	4.29	.46
No. of siblings	1.38	.90	1.44	1.05
Mean age of mother in years	34.7	5.42	34.8	4.83
Maternal education				
% 12 years or more	83.2		88.5	
% 10 years or less	14.42		8.64	
% 7 years or less	1.92		2.05	
% No schooling	.48		.82	
Mean age of father in years	36.8	5.64	37.12	5.49
Paternal education				
% 12 years or more	89.7		91.52	
% 10 years or less	6.7		7.14	
% 7 years or less	3.6		.89	
% No schooling	0		.45	
Birth order	1.8	1.11	1.9	1.04
% female	50.5		38.5	
% male	49.5		51.3	
% sole parent families	8.7		7.3	
% two parent families	88		76.9	
Conduct problems	6.9	1.8	6.8	1.6
Hyperactivity	8.4	2.32	8.4	2.34
Anxiety	6.5	1.6	6.6	1.6
Peer relationships	6.44	1.5	6.72	1.5
Pro-social behaviours	12.5	1.73	12.4	1.7
Parental involvement	39.9	4.5	39.6	5
Parental supervision	15.54	4.01	15.06	3.9
Positive parenting techniques	26.26	2.37	26	2.64
Parental inconsistent discipline	13.74	3.17	13.29	3.25
Parents use of corporal punishment	5.36	1.54	5.56	1.52

Stage One Screening

To determine participant suitability for the trial, classroom teachers involved in the study were asked to complete the screening stage one measure. A description outlining typical characteristics associated with a child with conduct problems was given and teachers were asked to classify those children who had received parental consent to participate in the study according to whether they were 'often like the child described', 'sometimes like the child described' or 'rarely like the child described'. Children who were classified as 'most' or 'sometimes' like the child described formed the 'indicated' cohort for the remainder of the study. The total number of children included in the indicated cohort following stage one of the screening process was 177. Of the 177 identified children, 80 were included in the EI group and 97 in the control group. Table 5 provides a summary of frequencies identified following the first stage of screening.

Stage Two Screening

For the second stage of screening teachers were asked to consult the list of indicated children identified in the first stage of screening to determine whether any of the students met exclusion criteria included on the stage two screening measure. Forty children were excluded based on the teacher's judgment concerning whether the child: spoke English as a second language; experienced problematic anxiety; showed evidence of language delays; experienced learning difficulties; was aged beyond the 4 to 5 year age limit for the study; suffered from a major illness; was diagnosed with Attention Deficit Disorder and/or; was medicated for Attention Deficit Disorder. Table 5 presents frequencies for the exclusion criteria considered for the second stage of screening.

There were no significant differences between the EI and control group for the final cohort of indicated children following screening. There was a relatively balanced gender distribution across the EI and control groups for the universal and indicated samples. Within the indicated sample, there was an over representation of boys, however, again the distribution of gender across the EI and control cohort was balanced.

Table 5.

Numbers and Percentages of Screening Stage One and Two Characteristics for Children (Indicated Sample)

Screening Characteristics – Stage One	Experimental		Control	
	n	*%*	*n*	*%*
Often like the child described	10	9.6	12	9.1
Sometimes like the child described	29	27.9	34	25.8
Rarely like the child described	65	62.5	86	65.2
Total	104	100	132	100
Screening Characteristics – Stage Two (Male)	*n*	*%*	*n*	*%*
English as a second language	5	4.8	1	.8
Problematic anxiety	0	0	4	3
Language delays	2	1.9	5	3.8
Learning difficulties	2	1.9	5	3.8
Age other than 4 or 5 years	0	0	0	0
Major illness	1	.9	0	0
Attention deficit disorder	0	0	0	0
Medicated for attention deficit disorder	0	0	0	0
Screening Characteristics – Stage One (Female)	Experimental		Control	
	n	*%*	*n*	*%*
Often like the child described	3	2.9	6	5.9
Sometimes like the child described	19	18.1	19	18.8
Rarely like the child described	83	79	76	75.2
Total	105	100	101	100
Screening Characteristics – Stage Two (Female)	*n*	*%*	*n*	*%*
English as a second language	2	1.9	0	0
Problematic anxiety	2	1.9	0	0
Language delays	2	1.9	0	0
Learning difficulties	4	3.8	1	1
Age other than 4 or 5 years	0	0	0	0
Major illness	1	.9	0	0
Attention deficit disorder	0	0	0	0
Medicated for attention deficit disorder	0	0	0	0

Treatment Integrity and Engagement

To determine implementation fidelity for teachers, parents, and the behaviour consultant involved in the facilitation of the EI program, treatment integrity and process measures were completed at post-intervention. A description of the levels of engagement at the school and home levels follows.

Teacher Engagement in the School Component of the EI Program

To measure participating teachers' levels of engagement in the EI program, the nine teachers assigned to the EI group completed the program implementation subscale of the Teacher Self Report at post-intervention (TSR). All participants selected the same category (80% to 100%) on six of the seven items. Overall percentages measuring teachers' levels of engagement throughout the intervention phase of the study are presented as follows: In the implementation and facilitation of the EI program, all teachers applied the strategies of management within the range as indicated by the highest end of the 5 point scale showing 80% to 100% consistency. All participating teachers endeavoured to include all students in the curriculum and associated activities within the range of 80% to 100% regularity. All teachers actively encouraged participating children to consider pro-social responses as an alternative to inappropriate behavioural choices as indicated by the scale of 80% to 100%. All EI teachers regularly delivered the EI Program curriculum within the range of 80% to 100%. Further, all teachers consistently adhered to the curriculum delivery guidelines within the indicated range of 80% to 100%. All participating teachers consistently encouraged each class member to actively participate in the curriculum component of the EI Program within the 80% to 100% range. Finally, 89% of teachers endeavoured to maintain regular contact with parents, where necessary, within the range of 80% to 100% consistency.

Behaviour Consultant Engagement in the EI Program

The Behaviour Consultant Self Report (BSR) was utilised to determine the behaviour consultant's level of engagement with indicated children in the EI group. The behaviour consultant selected the same category of response (80% to 100%) for all items. On the program implementation subscale of the BSR at post-intervention the behaviour consultant reported high levels of engagement. Overall percentages measuring the behaviour consultant's levels of engagement throughout the

58

intervention phase of the study are presented as follows: The consultant met with each indicated child on a weekly basis and recorded on a five point scale an 80% to 100% consistency. He regularly employed strategies that closely aligned with those developed for inclusion in the EI program design to facilitate program consistency within the range of 80% to 100%.

The consultant actively encouraged indicated children to consider pro-social responses as an alternative to inappropriate behavioural choices as indicated by the scale of 80% to 100%. In meeting with each child the behaviour consultant regularly referred to concepts explored in the program curriculum within the range of 80% to 100%. The consultant made regular weekly contact with each child's teacher in order to provide additional support for their management of the child and delivery of the program as indicated by the scale of 80% to 100%. Finally, the behaviour consultant consistently endeavoured to keep each child's parent informed regarding key concepts covered with the child in each session within the range of 80% to 100%.

Parent Engagement in Parent Training

As noted in the previous chapter, all parents in the EI cohort were invited to participate in three, two-hour parent training sessions. Seventy-two parents (34%) of the full EI cohort completed at least one session of training. Of the 72 parents, 37 parents (56%) of indicated children participated in either group training (at least one of the three sessions) or an individual session. Of the 37 indicated parents, 11 parents participated in one session of the group facilitated parent program, four parents in two sessions and 14 parents in three sessions. The remaining parents (eight) were invited to participate in a two hour, one-on-one training session with a parent – trainer who facilitated the individual sessions at the child's school or in the parent's home. Of the 35 parents (31%) of non-indicated children, 16 participated in one session of the group training, four parents attended two sessions and 15 parents participated in three sessions.

On the socio-demographic variables measuring mothers' and fathers' education levels and family income, there was a significant difference found between the cohort of parents who attended parent training and those who did not attend on the variable of the fathers' levels of education, $F(1,189)=5.30$, $p<.05$. Those fathers who did attend parent training indicated higher levels of educational attainment. On the variables measured on the subscales of the SDQ (Parent) and SDQ (Teacher) there were no significant differences found between the children whose parents engaged in parent training and those who did not attend the training sessions.

Parent Engagement in the Home Component of the EI Program

To measure participating parents' levels of confidence in implementing the home component of the EI program, the Parent Self Report (PSR) was administered at post intervention to all parents in the EI cohort who had completed at least one session of parent training during the implementation phase. A Cronbach α level (SPSS) of .85 was calculated on this measure indicating acceptable internal consistency. Forty-five parents completed the PSR with results indicating high levels of engagement in the implementation of the parenting program. Of the 45 parents who completed the parent self-report, 84% of parents either agreed or strongly agreed that, when disciplining their child, they felt confident using the strategies learnt through the parent training component (M=1.98, SD=.79). 76% of parents reported that they felt more confident about disciplining their child as a result of their attendance at the parent training program (M=2.2, SD=.79). 73% of parents indicated that they found the strategies they learnt as part of the training had helped them in the discipline of their child (M=2.20, SD=.69). 62% of parents also reported that, since attending the parent training, their ability to manage their child had improved (M=2.42, SD=.84). Finally, 93% of parents indicated that they had kept in touch with their child's teacher throughout the facilitation of the program, suggesting that the program design served to encourage stronger partnerships between parents and teachers (M=1.84, SD=.67).

Service Satisfaction

Teacher and parent participant satisfaction was measured using overall percentages taken from items on the TSR and PSR respectively at post-intervention. Of the nine teachers who engaged in the EI program, 62% strongly agreed and 37.5% agreed that the design of the EI Program provided a sound framework to assist in working more effectively with children exhibiting problem behaviour (M=1.38, SD=.52). 87.5% of teachers strongly agreed and 12.5% of teachers agreed that the EI Program provided further assistance for those children at-risk for the development of problem behaviours (M=1.13, SD=.35). 62.5% of teachers indicated that as a result of the class group's engagement in the EI program, children were well behaved for 80% to 100% of the time, while 37.5% reported that children were well behaved between

60% and 79% of the time (M=1.38, SD=.52). 75% of teachers indicated that that their ability to manage the class group was excellent, while 25% described their classroom management ability to be good (M=1.25, SD=.46). Finally, 50% of the EI teachers reported that children perceived to be more at-risk for ongoing behaviour problems were well behaved for 80% to 100% of the time (M=1.63, SD=.74). 37.5% indicated that the more at-risk children were well behaved for 60% to 79% of the time. 12.5% reported that indicated children exhibited pro-social behaviours for 40% to 59% of the time. These findings suggest that teachers were highly satisfied with the EI program as a means of working with children at-risk of problem behaviour in the classroom context.

Of the 45 parents who completed some parent training as part of the EI intervention, 11.1% strongly agreed and 62.2% agreed that strategies acquired through the program training assisted them in the discipline of their child (M=2.20, SD=.69). 62.2% of parents reported that, since participating in the parent training component of the intervention, their ability to manage their child's behaviour had improved (M=2.42, SD=.84).

Reliability of Outcome Measures

To determine the reliability of subscales on measures including the Alabama Parenting Questionnaire, Strengths and Difficulties Questionnaire (Parent and Teacher), and Peer Nominations Schedule, Cronbach α levels (SPSS) were calculated. Table 6 shows acceptable internal consistency except the measure of corporal punishment on the Alabama Parenting Questionnaire. Caution was exercised in interpreting this measure.

Interrater Agreement on Classroom Observations

In the EI investigation, interrater reliability was checked on the Classroom Observation Measure by having teacher aides trained in the observation process complete 100% of the observations concurrently with the classroom teachers at pre, post and six-month follow-up. Correlations between scores obtained from the teachers and teacher aides engaged in the observation process were taken at pre-intervention and calculated for each variable on the Classroom Observation Measure. Correlations were considered significant at the .01 level. The correlation on each

Table 6.

Reliability Analysis of Outcome Measures

Scale	Cronbach α
Alabama Parenting Questionnaire:	
Parent involvement	.78
Parental supervision	.69
Positive parenting techniques	.71
Inconsistent discipline	.73
Corporal punishment	.45
Strengths and Difficulties Questionnaire (Teacher):	
Conduct problems	.73
Hyperactivity	.88
Anxiety	.75
Peer relationships	.58
Pro-social behaviours	.86
Strengths and Difficulties Questionnaire (Parent):	
Conduct problems	.59
Hyperactivity	.77
Anxiety	.56
Peer relationships	.50
Pro-social behaviours	.59
Peer Nominations Schedule:	
Negative Peer Interaction	.87

variable were: (a) .27 (off task behaviour); (b) .51 (disrespectfulness); (c) .29 (failure to follow directions); (d) .55 (physical and verbal aggression); and (e) .73 (group behaviour). These correlations, while low, indicate adequate reliability on the variables of the classroom observation measure.

Interrater Agreement on Diagnoses

Interrater reliability on clinical diagnoses for this study was checked by having two diagnosticians make independent assessments on 20% of the interviews. Results at the p<0.01 level were accepted as statistically significant. Correlations between scores obtained from the diagnostic interviews for the highest rate of severity on the independent assessments were significant at the level of .97. Of the 20% (n=28) of independent assessments, there was 100% agreement between the diagnosticians on whether diagnosis or no diagnosis was met. Twenty of the child participants were given no diagnosis, and 8 of the participants a diagnosis based on both independent assessments at the six-month follow-up period.

Correlations Comparing Perceptions of Disturbance in Children

To examine whether teachers, parents, children and diagnosticians agreed on behavioural disturbance in children at six-month follow-up, correlations were determined based on the SDQ (Teacher), SDQ (Parent), Peer Nominations Schedule and the DISCAP. Correlations were considered significant at the .01 level. The correlation between peer and parent perceptions was significant at .20. There was a significant correlation between peer and teacher perceptions at a level of .36. However, the correlation between the peer and diagnostician perceptions was non-significant at -.04. The correlation between parent and teacher perceptions was significant at .32. There was also a correlation between parent and diagnostician perceptions at a level of .19. The correlation between teacher and diagnostician perceptions was not significant at .15. While the majority of correlations were significant at the .01 level, no correlation was above .4. However, these correlations indicate adequate reliability on teacher, parent, child and diagnostician perceptions regarding disturbances in children at the six-month follow-up period.

Effectiveness of the EI Program

The author initially used Hierarchical Linear Modelling (HLM) as a means of assessing the effectiveness of the EI program. HLM provides a method of analysis that recognises the hierarchy of particular data structures (Bryk & Raudenbush, 2002). This approach utilises statistical techniques that take hierarchical data structures into account. Bryk and Raudenbush (2002) state that '...behavioral and social data commonly have a nested structure, including, for example, repeated observations nested within persons. These persons also may be nested within organizational units such as schools. Further, the organizational units themselves may be nested within communities, within states, and even within countries' (p. 6). HLM allows for the analysis of data grouped according to particular hierarchical levels in a way that minimises aggregation bias, mis-estimated precision and other related issues associated with units of analysis.

In terms of the investigation, variables were clustered according to levels pertaining to the individual (level one), and class/school (level two), and this method of statistical analysis was considered to be appropriate. The statistical software package (HLM 6) (Bryk, Raudenbush, & Congdon, 2004) was utilised to run the analysis. Thus, the main outcome variable of the SDQ total score was used as a dependent variable. At level-1, ordinary-least-squares methods were used to generate a slope for each child's SDQ score regressed against the three time points. Intercepts and slopes for SDQ scores were then used as dependent variables to be modelled against level-2 variables of intervention versus control group, class size, school size, parent training attendance rates, and teacher experience. HLM partitions variance into the various levels and the intra-class correlation, a ratio of level-2 variance over level-1 plus level-2 variance, reflects the extent to which explanatory variance exists at level-2. For the slopes of SDQ, the intra-class correlation for level-2 effects was (.001 / .001 + 23.93 = < .001), indicating that the second level variables had no significant effect upon child slopes. Consistent with this, no coefficients for level-2 variables were significantly related to SDQ slopes (intervention group: coeff = .114, SE = .118; school size: .00003, SE = .0002; Teacher's experience: coeff = .011, SE = .007; percentage of parents attending parent training in each school PT: coeff = .0063, SE = .008 – all $p > .15$).

Thus, all further analyses were conducted at the child level of analysis using traditional MANOVA techniques. Given that measures on child behaviour and

64

teaching and parent management were taken from participants involved in the study over time and correlated, repeated measures multivariate analyses of variance (MANOVA) were therefore used to test differences between each group from baseline to six-month follow-up. Where significant time differences, group and interaction effects were found, bonferroni tests were used to locate the source of the interactions at the accepted alpha level of .05.

Child Behaviour – School Level

To examine the effects of the intervention at both the home and school for child behaviour, the Teacher Strengths and Difficulties Questionnaire (SDQ (Teacher)), Classroom Observation Measure (Larmar & Dadds, 2002), and the Parent Strengths and Difficulties Questionnaire (SDQ) were administered and analysed at pre-, post, and six-month follow-up.

Teacher SDQ Reports – Full Sample. Two repeated measures multivariate analyses of variance (MANOVA) with the between participants factors of group (EI, and Control Group), and within participants factor of time (pre-intervention, post-intervention, and follow-up) were conducted for the full sample on the core measures of Conduct Problem (CP) and Hyperactivity (H) and the auxiliary measures of Anxiety (ANX), Peer Relationships (PR), and Pro-social (PRO) on the Teacher Strengths and Difficulties Questionnaire (SDQ (Teacher)) respectively. Table 7 shows means and standard deviations for SDQ (Teacher) – CP, SDQ (Teacher) – H, SDQ (Teacher) – ANX, SDQ (Teacher) – PR, and SDQ (Teacher) – PR at pre, post, and follow-up. The MANOVA for core measures showed main effects for group, $F(2, 236)=4.28, p<.05$, time, $F(4, 234)=16.07, p<.01$, and the interaction, $F(4, 234)=2.48, p<.05$. Follow-up univariate analyses showed the interaction was significant for both CP and H. Bonferonni tests were used to locate the source of the interactions. As can be seen from Table 7, the two groups were not different for the CP and H subscales at pre-, diverged at post- and were significantly different, with the EI group showing lower levels of CP and H. At follow-up the EI group appears to maintain its relative gains, however, the difference was no longer significant.

For the measures of ANX, PR, and PRO, the MANOVA revealed main effects for group, $F(3, 226)=11.88, p<.01$, time $F(6, 223)=23.80, p<.01$, and the interaction, $F(6, 223)=5.94, p<.01$. Follow-up univariate analyses showed the interaction was

65

significant for ANX, PR, and PRO. Table 7 indicates that the two groups for the PR subscale were not different at pre-, diverge at post- and were significantly different, and remained different at follow-up but were not significant. For the PRO subscale, the two groups are not different at pre-, diverge at post- and are significantly different and continue to be significantly different at follow-up. For the ANX subscale, the two groups are not different at pre-, diverge at post but are not significantly different, and then reach a level of significant difference in scores at follow-up.

Teacher SDQ Reports – Indicated Sample. The same MANOVAS were repeated using the smaller indicated sample with the between participants factors of group (EI, and Control Group), and within participants factor of time (pre-intervention, post-intervention, and follow-up) on the core variables of CP and H and the auxiliary variables of ANX, PR, and PRO respectively. Table 7 shows means and standard deviations for SDQ (Teacher) – CP, SDQ (Teacher) – H, SDQ (Teacher) – ANX, SDQ (Teacher) – PR, and SDQ (Teacher) – PR scores at pre-, post-, and follow-up. Results were first analysed on dependent measures of CP and H using 2 (group: EI versus Control) x 3 (time: pre, post, fu) MANOVA. The MANOVA showed no main effects for group $F(2, 134)=1.11$, $p>.05$, a main effect for time $F(4, 132)=14.49$, $p<.01$, and an interaction, $F(4, 132)=2.72$, $p<.05$. Follow-up univariate analyses showed the interaction was significant for both CP and H. Results from Table 7 show the two groups are not different for the CP and H subscales at pre-, diverge at post- and remain different at follow-up; however, the bonferonni tests failed to find significant differences at either point using its extra conservative criteria.

For the measures of ANX, PR, and PRO, the MANOVA revealed main effects for group, $F(3, 125)=5.72$, $p<.01$, time $F(6, 122)=18.56$, $p<.01$, and the interaction, $F(6, 122)=3.87$, $p<.01$. Follow-up univariate analyses showed the interaction was significant for PR and PRO. Table 7 indicates that the two groups for the PRO subscale are not different at pre-, diverge at post- and are significantly different, remain different at follow-up but no longer have significantly different scores. The two groups for the PR subscales are not different at pre-, diverge at post but are not significantly different, and remain not significant at follow-up.

Classroom Observation Measure Reports – Universal Sample. For the variables of off-task behaviour (OFTASK), disrespectfulness (DISRES), failure to follow directions (DIRECT), physical and verbal aggression (AGGRES), group behaviour (BEHAVE), and teacher confidence (CONFID) on the Classroom Observation Measure, two repeated measures multivariate analysis of variance (MANOVA) with the between participants factors of group (EI versus Control), and repeated measures factor of time (pre-intervention, post-intervention, and follow-up) were conducted. Table 8 shows means and standard deviations scores for the Classroom Observation Measure at pre-, post-, and follow-up. The MANOVA showed no main effects for group, $F(5, 8)=1.27$, $p>.05$, no main effect for time, $F(10, 3)=1.63$, $p>.05$, and no interaction.

Parenting Practices

Parent APQ Reports – Universal Sample. Two repeated measures multivariate analysis of variance (MANOVA) with the between participants factors of group (EI, and Control Group), and within participants factor of time (pre-intervention, post-intervention, and follow-up) was conducted on each subscale of the Alabama Parenting Questionnaire (APQ) for the entire cohort of participants. The variables included Parent Involvement (INVOL), Parent Supervision (PSUP), Positive Parenting Techniques (PPT) Inconsistent Discipline (INDIS), and Corporal Punishment (COPUN). Table 9 shows means and standard deviations at pre, post, and follow-up. The MANOVA for the five variables showed no main effects for group, $F(5, 224)=2.09$, $p>.05$, main effects for time, $F(10, 219)=4.97$, $p<.01$, and no interaction, $F(10, 219)=1.45$, $p>.05$. On each variable the time effects reflected small but consistent decreases on measures over time.

Parent APQ Reports – Treatment Sample versus Full Control Sample. The same MANOVA were repeated using the sample whose parents had received the intervention treatment and the full control sample with the between participants factors of group (EI – Treatment Sample, and Control Group), and within participants factor of time (pre-intervention, post-intervention, and follow-up) on each subscale of the Alabama Parenting Questionnaire. Table 9 shows means and standard deviations at pre, post, and follow-up. The MANOVA for the five variables showed no main effects for group, $F(5, 157)=.69$, $p>.05$, main effects for time, $F(10, 152)=2.61$, $p<.01$, and no interaction, $F(10, 152)=.64$, $p>.05$. Again, on each variable the time effects reflected small but consistent decreases on measures over time.

Parent APQ Reports – Indicated Sample. Two repeated measures multivariate analysis of variance (MANOVA) was also conducted on each subscale of the Alabama Parenting Questionnaire (APQ) for the indicated sample with the between participants factors of group (EI – Intention to Treat, and Control Group – Indicated), and within participants factor of time (pre-intervention, post-intervention, and follow-up). Table 9 shows means and standard deviations at pre, post, and follow-up. The MANOVA for the five variables showed main effects for group, $F(5, 72)=3.96$, $p<.01$, no main effects for time, $F(10, 67)=1.55$, $p>.05$, and no interaction, $F(10, 67)=.97$, $p>.05$. On each variable the group effects reflected small but consistent decreases on measures over time.

Child Behaviour – Home Level

　　Parent SDQ Reports – Universal Sample. Two repeated measures multivariate analysis of variance (MANOVA) with the between participants factors of group (EI, and Control Group), and within participants factor of time (pre-intervention, post-intervention, and follow-up) for the full sample was conducted on each subscale of the Parent Strengths and Difficulties Questionnaire (SDQ) including the core variables of Conduct Problem (CP), Hyperactivity (H), and the auxiliary variables of Anxiety (ANX), Peer Relationships (PR) and, Pro-social (PRO). Table 10 shows means and standard deviations at pre, post, and follow-up. The MANOVA for core variables showed no main effects for group, $F(2, 349)=.09$, $p>.05$, main effects for time, $F(4, 347)=6.71$, $p<.01$, and no interaction, $F(4, 347)=.60$, $p>.05$. For the measures of ANX, PR, and PRO, the MANOVA showed no main effects for group, $F(3, 330)=1.93$, $p>.01$, main effects for time, $F(6, 327)=4.66$, $p<.01$, and no interaction, $F(6, 327)=1.60$, $p>.05$. On all measures the time effects reflected small but consistent decreases on measures over time.

　　Parent SDQ Reports – Indicated Sample. The same MANOVA was repeated using the indicated sample with the between participants factors of group (EI, and Control Group), and within participants factor of time (pre-intervention, post-intervention, and follow-up) on each subscale of the Parent Strengths and Difficulties Questionnaire including core and auxiliary variables. Table 10 shows means and standard deviations at pre-, post-, and follow-up. The MANOVA for core variables showed no main effects for group, $F(2, 106)=.21$, $p>.05$, main effects for time, $F(4,$

104)=2.82, $p<.05$, and no interaction, $F(4, 104)=.74$, $p>.05$. Results were then analysed on auxiliary variables with the MANOVA showing no main effects for group, $F(3, 94)=1.88$, $p>.05$, main effects for time, $F(6, 91)=2.85$, $p<.01$, and no interaction, $F(6, 91)=1.52$, $p>.05$. Again, on all measures the time effects reflected small but consistent decreases on measures over time.

Peer Relationships

Peer Nomination Reports – Universal Sample. Two repeated measures multivariate analysis of variance (MANOVA) with the between participants factors of group (EI, and Control Group), and within participants factor of time (pre-intervention, post-intervention, and follow-up) for the entire cohort of participants was conducted on the variables of the Peer Nominations Schedule (PNS). Table 11 shows means and standard deviations for the variables' scores at pre, post, and follow-up. The MANOVA showed no main effects for time, $F(2, 506)=.82$, $p>.05$, and no interaction, $F(2, 506)=.29$, $p>.05$.

Peer Nomination Reports – Indicated Sample. The same MANOVA were repeated using the indicated sample with the between participants factors of group (EI, and Control Group), and within participants factor of time (pre-intervention, post-intervention, and follow-up) on the variables of the PSN. Table 11 shows means and standard deviations for the variables' scores at pre-, post-, and follow-up. The MANOVA showed no main effects for time, $F(2, 174)=.58$, $p>.05$, and no interaction, $F(2, 174)=1.65$, $p>.05$.

Diagnostic Data

Table 12 shows the follow-up clinical status of the indicated participants in the study. At the 6-month follow-up period Chi-square analyses showed there were no significant differences between the EI and control group for any diagnosis, $\chi^2(1, N=136)=1.10$, $p=.213$, internalising diagnosis, $\chi^2(1, N=134)=3.77$, $p=.063$, and externalising diagnosis, $\chi^2(1, N=134)=.094$, $p=.519$.

69

Table 7. Means and Standard Deviations for the Teacher Strengths and Difficulties Questionnaire's Core and Auxiliary Variables at Pre-intervention, Post-intervention and Follow-up (Full and Indicated Samples)

	EI GROUP (FULL SAMPLE)						CONTROL GROUP (FULL SAMPLE)					
	Pre		Post		F-up		Pre		Post		F-up	
	M	SD	M	SD	M	SD	M	SD	M	SD	M	SD
CP	6.36	1.89	5.59	1.12	5.65	1.23	6.51	1.63	6.24	1.55	6.10	1.78
H	8.46	3.02	6.91	2.52	6.97	2.41	8.88	2.66	8.16	2.87	7.96	3.03
ANX	6.12	1.60	5.75	1.64	5.43	.89	5.92	1.43	5.97	1.71	5.93	1.64
PR	6.49	1.50	5.68	1.08	5.62	1.18	6.67	1.63	6.44	1.60	6.10	1.49
PRO	11.67	2.34	13.71	1.94	13.40	2.21	10.49	2.33	11.53	2.51	11.92	2.91

	EI GROUP (INDICATED SAMPLE)						CONTROL GROUP (INDICATED SAMPLE)					
	Pre		Post		F-up		Pre		Post		F-up	
	M	SD	M	SD	M	SD	M	SD	M	SD	M	SD
CP	7.33	2.06	5.98	1.33	6.05	1.52	7.16	1.65	6.65	1.67	6.49	2.06
H	10.03	2.96	7.90	2.85	7.88	2.72	9.81	2.48	8.88	2.98	8.84	3.13
ANX	6.25	1.88	6.04	2.07	5.47	.99	6.13	1.49	5.86	1.53	5.79	1.38
PR	6.98	1.59	6.02	1.28	5.91	1.39	6.80	1.59	6.50	1.50	6.29	1.55
PRO	10.36	2.06	13.11	2.12	12.66	2.48	9.71	1.90	10.93	2.56	11.29	3.11

Note: *CP* SDQ Conduct Problem; *H* SDQ Hyperactivity; *ANX* SDQ Anxiety; *PR* SDQ Peer Relationships; and *Pro-social Behaviour Sub-scales.*

Table 8. Means and Standard Deviations for the Classroom Observation Measure Variables at Pre-intervention, Post-intervention and Follow-up (Full Sample)

| | EI GROUP (FULL SAMPLE) | | | | | | CONTROL GROUP (FULL SAMPLE) | | | | | |
| | Pre | | Post | | F-up | | Pre | | Post | | F-up | |
	M	SD	M	SD	M	SD	M	SD	M	SD	M	SD
OFTASK	3.54	.56	3.67	.80	3.75	.41	3.64	.33	3.61	.36	3.76	.29
DISRES	4.68	.36	4.77	.24	4.77	.24	4.51	.42	4.41	.41	4.50	.47
DIRECT	3.44	.35	3.55	.70	3.82	.52	3.67	.37	3.61	.28	3.70	.42
AGGRES	4.39	.43	4.66	.35	4.38	.49	4.08	.50	4.11	.31	4.31	.40
BEHAVE	2.16	.21	1.81	.46	2.02	.33	2.28	.38	2.09	.55	1.97	.50
CONFID												

Note: OFTASK= Off task behaviour; DIRES= Disrespectfulness; DIRECT= Failure to follow directions; AGGRES= Physical and verbal aggression; BEHAVE= Group behaviour; and CONFID= Teacher confidence.

Table 9. Means and Standard Deviations for the Parent Strengths and Difficulties Questionnaire's Core and Auxiliary Variables at Pre-intervention, Post-intervention and Follow-up (Full and Indicated Samples)

EI GROUP (FULL SAMPLE)

	Pre		Post		F-up	
	M	SD	M	SD	M	SD
CP	6.79	1.61	6.53	1.59	6.46	1.52
H	8.23	2.23	8.06	2.28	7.96	2.13
ANX	6.41	1.50	6.41	1.59	6.27	1.42
PR	6.34	1.44	6.28	1.45	6.16	1.35
PRO	12.58	1.70	12.88	1.69	13.06	1.80

CONTROL GROUP (FULL SAMPLE)

	Pre		Post		F-up	
	M	SD	M	SD	M	SD
CP	6.72	1.53	6.55	1.63	6.37	1.59
H	8.34	2.25	7.98	2.31	7.96	2.35
ANX	6.44	1.49	6.24	1.37	6.29	1.40
PR	6.67	1.43	6.24	1.32	6.26	1.26
PRO	12.38	1.61	12.51	1.80	12.60	1.82

EI GROUP (INDICATED SAMPLE)

	Pre		Post		F-up	
	M	SD	M	SD	M	SD
CP	7.34	1.59	6.87	1.69	6.68	1.49
H	9.06	2.37	8.91	2.54	8.55	2.12
ANX	6.22	1.44	6.02	1.10	6.13	1.38
PR	6.42	1.34	6.29	1.20	6.02	1.29
PRO	12.09	1.52	12.76	1.51	12.96	1.75

CONTROL GROUP (INDICATED SAMPLE)

	Pre		Post		F-up	
	M	SD	M	SD	M	SD
CP	7.23	1.52	7.05	1.76	7.02	1.83
H	9.19	2.21	9.10	2.39	9.00	2.51
ANX	6.40	1.46	6.32	1.53	6.15	1.51
PR	6.83	1.49	6.47	1.62	6.45	1.32
PRO	11.83	1.68	12.08	1.79	11.92	2.11

Note: CP–SDQ Conduct Problem; H–SDQ Hyperactivity; ANX–SDQ Anxiety; PR–SDQ Peer Relationships; and Pro-social Behaviour Sub-scales.

Table 10. Means and Standard Deviations for the Alabama Parenting Questionnaire's Subscales at Pre-intervention, Post-intervention and Follow-up (Full, Indicated- Treatment, Indicated – Intention to Treat Samples)

EI GROUP (FULL SAMPLE)

	Pre		Post		F-up	
	M	SD	M	SD	M	SD
INVOL	39.95	4.00	40.26	3.70	41.26	7.16
PSUP	15.27	3.77	15.07	3.92	15.70	5.73
PPT	26.17	2.41	25.90	2.47	25.66	2.70
INDIS	13.59	3.17	13.46	3.00	13.94	3.36
COPU	5.41	1.55	5.08	1.62	5.04	1.48

CONTROL GROUP (FULL SAMPLE)

	Pre		Post		F-up	
	M	SD	M	SD	M	SD
INVOL	39.70	4.43	39.72	4.25	39.68	3.97
PSUP	14.85	3.42	15.29	4.11	14.64	3.21
PPT	25.81	2.60	25.82	2.43	25.50	2.46
INDIS	13.02	3.08	12.99	3.30	12.85	3.24
COPU	5.57	1.44	5.28	1.54	5.06	1.39

EI GROUP (INDICATED – TREATMENT SAMPLE)

	Pre		Post		F-up	
	M	SD	M	SD	M	SD
INVOL	40.73	4.03	40.90	3.71	40.95	4.04
PSUP	14.90	3.75	14.63	3.14	14.29	3.04
PPT	26.41	2.45	26.10	2.37	25.51	2.68
INDIS	12.59	2.89	12.54	2.92	12.85	3.25
COPU	5.17	1.45	5.05	1.69	5.05	1.50

CONTROL GROUP (FULL SAMPLE)

	Pre		Post		F-up	
	M	SD	M	SD	M	SD
INVOL	39.70	4.43	39.72	4.25	39.68	3.97
PSUP	14.85	3.42	15.29	4.11	14.64	3.21
PPT	25.81	2.60	25.82	2.43	25.50	2.46
INDIS	13.02	3.08	12.99	3.30	12.85	3.24
COPU	5.57	1.44	5.28	1.54	5.06	1.39

EI GROUP (INDICATED – INTENTION TO TREAT SAMPLE)

	Pre		Post		F-up	
	M	SD	M	SD	M	SD
INVOL	40.49	3.59	40.94	3.00	41.20	3.48
PSUP	16.31	4.36	15.60	4.19	15.06	3.80
PPT	26.17	2.27	26.49	2.16	26.06	2.46
INDIS	13.40	2.90	12.94	3.18	13.26	3.45
COPU	5.74	1.65	5.49	1.96	5.31	1.62

CONTROL GROUP (INDICATED SAMPLE)

	Pre		Post		F-up	
	M	SD	M	SD	M	SD
INVOL	38.12	4.58	37.95	4.55	38.07	3.87
PSUP	14.74	3.30	15.98	4.98	14.91	3.10
PPT	25.56	2.80	25.47	2.99	25.74	2.63
INDIS	13.51	3.09	13.60	3.44	13.42	3.63
COPU	5.79	1.44	5.60	1.37	5.26	1.40

Note: INVOL=APQ Parent Involvement; PSUP=APQ Parent Supervision; PPT=APQ Positive Parenting Techniques; INDIS=APQ Inconsistent Discipline; and COPU(N=)APQ Corporal Punishment Sub-scales.

Table 11. Means and Standard Deviations for the Peer Nominations Schedule at Pre-intervention, Post-intervention and Follow-up (Universal and Indicated Samples)

	EI GROUP (UNIVERSAL SAMPLE)						CONTROL GROUP (UNIVERSAL SAMPLE)					
	Pre		Post		F-up		Pre		Post		F-up	
	M	SD	M	SD	M	SD	M	SD	M	SD	M	SD
PEER	3.39	6.13	3.90	8.18	3.61	8.16	3.93	7.16	4.05	7.68	3.93	7.92

	EI GROUP (INDICATED SAMPLE)						CONTROL GROUP (INDICATED SAMPLE)					
	Pre		Post		F-up		Pre		Post		F-up	
	M	SD	M	SD	M	SD	M	SD	M	SD	M	SD
PEER	4.65	8.67	6.12	11.37	6.44	11.32	6.81	10.39	6.45	10.98	6.31	10.86

Note: PEER= Negative Peer Interactions

74

Table 12

Diagnostic Data at 6-month Follow-up

	EI Group (*n*=60) %	Control Group (*n*=76) %
Children with:		
Any diagnosis	16.7%	10.5%
Internalising diagnosis	8.3%	1.4%
Externalising diagnosis	6.7%	5.4%
Attention Deficit Hyperactivity Disorder	5%	2.7%
Enuresis	6.7%	5.3%
Separation Anxiety Disorder	1.7%	2.7%
Oppositional Defiant Disorder	3.3%	6.7%
Social Phobia	1.7%	2.7%
Specific Phobia	8.3%	6.7%
Adjustment Disorder	1.7%	4%
Encopresis	0%	4%
School Refusal	3.3%	0%
Conduct Disorder	1.7%	1%
Major Depressive Disorder	1.7%	0%
Depressive Disorder	0%	1.3%

Severity Rating. ANOVA (SPSS) was used to test the significance of differences between mean scores for the highest severity rating of diagnosis at six-months follow-up. Results at the .05 level were accepted as statistically significant. The mean and standard deviation scores for the EI group on the highest rating of severity were $\underline{M}$=.77 and $\underline{SD}$=1.43. For the control group the mean and standard deviation scores for the highest severity rating were $\underline{M}$=.45 and $\underline{SD}$=.99. The ANOVA detected no statistically significant differences for group $F(1,132)$=2.38, p>.05 at the six-month follow-up period.

This chapter has provided a summary of the findings that emerged from the EI program evaluation. The following chapter focuses discussion on the findings of the study, strengths and limitations of the research design, and considers the implications of the investigation on future research and practice in early intervention and prevention.

Chapter 5: Discussion and Conclusions

The aim of the Early Impact Program investigation was to evaluate the implementation and efficacy of an early intervention and prevention program for children at-risk for conduct problems. The first aim centred upon the social validity of the program to determine whether the EI program could be implemented with sound program fidelity within regular school communities. The second hypothesis sought to determine whether the EI program's multi-modal intervention framework would reduce the incidence of problem behaviour and encourage pro-social responses in pre-school aged children at the home and school level.

From the first hypothesis a guiding question was formulated that focussed on whether the program could be implemented in a school community setting by teachers in regular preschool classes. From the second hypothesis, five research questions were developed to guide the study and tested to determine their outcomes. The first question was whether the school component of the program reduced the incidence of problem behaviour in children in the school setting. The second question considered whether the school component influenced greater pro-social responses in children in the school context. The third question was directed towards the home environment and whether there was a decrease in parents' use of aversive parenting strategies as a result of parents' engagement in the program. The fourth question was directed towards whether the home component of the program served to reduce problem behaviours in children in the home setting. The fifth question was concerned with whether there was an increase in pro-social behaviours in children in the home setting as a result of the home component of the program. The following section provides discussion focussing on the outcomes of the research questions formulated for the study as a means of determining the effectiveness of the EI Program's implementation.

Social Validity of the EI Program

The first hypothesis examined in the EI study focussed on the following research question: 'Would the EI program targeting children and families at-risk of conduct problems demonstrate high social validity as reflected by: (a) high participation rates; (b) high retention rates; and (c) high satisfaction rates?'

Levels of Engagement

Child Participation. One of the measures to determine the social validity of the EI program was the level of participation in the research. The rate of children recruited into the study was high with 80% of parents from the participating preschool cohorts consenting to their child's participation. This high rate of participation reflected parents' interest in the focus of the research and enthusiasm for their child's involvement in the program.

Teacher Participation. Of the nine teachers involved in the implementation and facilitation of the EI program, all teachers were actively engaged throughout the implementation period. All teachers indicated that they consistently applied the strategies of management to their respective class group throughout the implementation process. All teachers reported that they endeavoured to include all students in the curriculum and associated activities during the implementation of the intervention. Participating teachers indicated that they consistently assisted in encouraging participating children to consider pro-social responses as an alternative to inappropriate behavioural choices. All teachers reported that they consistently delivered the EI Program curriculum throughout the intensive and extended phase of the intervention. Further, participating teachers consistently adhered to the curriculum delivery guidelines during the implementation process. All teachers regularly encouraged class members to actively participate in the curriculum component of the EI Program. Finally, all teachers maintained regular contact with parents throughout the duration of the intervention. Such high levels of engagement indicate that teachers were implementing the program with high treatment fidelity. Further, these findings would indicate that the program design allows for ease of facilitation in the regular school classroom context.

All teachers reported high levels of satisfaction with the program as discussed in a later section of this book, further reflecting teacher perceptions regarding the utility and social validity of the school component of the EI program.

Parent Participation. The general level of parent engagement in the EI parenting component of the program was promising for prevention studies with 30.5% of parents in the EI cohort of schools participating. However, for the cohort of parents whose children were identified as more at-risk for ongoing behaviour problems the participation rates were low. This trend is worthy of discussion given that it is common for this type of intervention. Parents identified as having the greatest need for parenting assistance often fail to engage in community and school based parenting programs (Spoth et al., 1999; Spoth et al., 1996). Existing models of treatment are primarily clinic and community based and therefore fail to adequately target this population despite the accessibility of such programs in regular community settings. Such a trend highlights the need to develop alternative programs designed to more effectively reach this target group. Despite lower attendance rates for this cohort, the full sample generally reported high levels of satisfaction with the program as reported in a later section.

Behaviour Consultant Participation. The behaviour consultant involved in the facilitation of the indicated component of the study reported high levels of engagement. The consultant regularly met with each indicated child on a weekly basis throughout the intensive and extended phase of the intervention. He facilitated program consistency by employing strategies that aligned with those included in the EI program design. The consultant reported that he consistently encouraged indicated children to consider pro-social responses as an alternative to inappropriate behavioural choices. Throughout the implementation process the behaviour consultant regularly referred to concepts explored in the program curriculum. The consultant maintained weekly contact with each child's teacher in order to provide additional support for their management of the child and delivery of the program. Finally, the behaviour consultant consistently endeavoured to keep each child's parent informed regarding key concepts covered with the child in each session. The behaviour consultant's reported levels of engagement indicate consistently high participation rates for the behaviour consultant involved in the implementation process suggesting high implementation fidelity.

Retention in the Study

Another factor indicating the social validity of the study was the high retention rates throughout the evaluation. The attrition rate from pre- to post- intervention was 99%, and 96% from pre-intervention to follow-up. No parent whose child remained enrolled in participating schools during the course of the investigation withdrew their child from participation in the study indicating their support for the child's involvement.

Service Satisfaction

The final indicator to determine the social validity of the EI program was participants' reported levels of satisfaction with the program design. A likely explanation for the promising retention rates of children and families throughout the study is that high participant satisfaction with the EI program contributed to parent's willingness for their child to participate. The following section provides discussion relating to teacher, parent and the behaviour consultant's levels of satisfaction with the program.

Teacher Satisfaction. Of the nine teachers involved in the implementation of the program all reported high levels of satisfaction with the EI program design. Throughout the initial recruitment and training process, teachers expressed enthusiasm for the program design and for their participation in the research. Many of the teachers commented that they thought their participation in the trial would be an effective way of helping others and investing into the school community. Teachers expressed the belief that early intervention and prevention programs were vital to the health of schools and the broader community. The majority of teachers also indicated that their participation in the program implementation training was useful in assisting them to reflect on their current approaches to managing children's behaviours. Further, teacher participants also commented that the training helped them to consider some of the dimensions surrounding problem behaviours in children and the most effective ways for working with children and families at-risk of conduct problems. Finally, all teachers reported that the EI program contributed to the promotion of positive behaviours for young children.

In terms of teacher engagement in the facilitation of the EI program a number of key factors were considered to determine program utility and fidelity. Specifically, when dealing with the class group each teacher reported low perceived levels of stress throughout the duration of the program facilitation. In applying the management strategies and curriculum to the class groups all teachers reported high levels of confidence. All teachers described their ability to manage the class group as either good or excellent. All teachers strongly agreed that the design of the EI Program provided a framework to assist them in working more effectively with children exhibiting problem behaviours. Finally, all teachers strongly agreed that the EI program provided further assistance for those children at-risk for the development of problem behaviours.

These reported levels of satisfaction with the EI program would indicate that the program design allows for ease of implementation and provides an easily disseminable framework that assists teachers in confidently managing classroom behaviour. Further, the teachers' responses would also suggest that the program assists teachers in providing remedial assistance for children more at-risk for ongoing behaviour problems.

Parent Satisfaction. Of the 45 parents who completed the parent self-report, 84% of parents either agreed or strongly agreed that, when disciplining their child, they felt confident using the strategies learnt through the parent training component. 76% of parents reported that they felt more confident about disciplining their child as a result of their attendance at the parent training program. 62% of parents indicated that they found the strategies they learnt as part of the training had helped them in the discipline of their child. 62% of parents also reported that, since attending the parent training, their ability to manage their child had improved. Finally, 93% of parents indicated that they had kept in touch with their child's teacher throughout the facilitation of the program, suggesting that the program design served to encourage stronger partnerships between parents and teachers. The levels of satisfaction reported by participating parents would suggest that the majority of parents found the parenting component of the program to be of benefit. Many indicated that they had developed greater confidence in the parenting role as a result of their engagement in the EI parent training program.

Behaviour Consultant's Satisfaction. It would seem that the behaviour consultant involved in the indicated component of the EI program was satisfied with the program design based on the reported levels of confidence in administering the program to the indicated cohort of EI participants. The consultant's rate of confidence in providing additional support to each child throughout the program was high, reporting confidence levels between 80% to 100%.

In summary, the rates of participation, retention, and levels of satisfaction throughout the trial support the social validity and utility of the EI program and demonstrated participants' support for an early intervention and prevention program targeting children and families at-risk of conduct problems. A high percentage of families consented to their child's participation in the research, with teachers and parents showing commitment to the implementation process. Retention rates were very promising with few child participants withdrawing from the study. Finally, levels of satisfaction with the EI program were high with the majority of participants indicating that the program provided benefit to the school communities involved in the study. The following section provides discussion focussing on outcomes associated with the second hypothesis for the study.

Effectiveness of the EI Program

The second hypothesis centred upon the efficacy of the EI program as an early intervention and prevention model of treatment to arrest the development of conduct problems in children. It was hypothesised that participation in the EI program would: (a) lower rates of problem behaviour in children at the school level; (b) increase pro-social responses in children at the school level; (c) reduce the rates of conduct problems in children at the home level; (d) increase the incidence of pro-social behaviours in children in the home setting; and (e) decrease the rates of aversive parenting practices at six-month follow-up.

Intervention Effects at the School Level

Reduction in Problem Behaviours. With regard to intervention effects, it was expected that the EI group would be associated with fewer conduct problems at the school level at post-intervention and follow-up compared with the control group. It was also expected that there would be greater effects for the indicated group in comparison to the full sample. It was held that the children's engagement in the curriculum and the teacher's management of the class group would serve to reduce the incidence of problem behaviours in the classroom. In terms of the findings of the first research question, there was a significant difference between scores on the core variables measuring conduct problems on the SDQ (Teacher) at post-intervention compared to the control group for the full sample. The extent of these differences in scores over time was accounted for by a reduction in mean values for the full sample of children in the EI group between pre- and post-intervention. This intervention effect marked a reduction in the symptoms of problem behaviour for the full sample that was sustained at post-intervention. However, while scores for the full sample of the EI group were maintained at six-month follow-up, the difference was no longer significant. For the indicated sample differences between groups in scores on the core variables measuring conduct problems at post-intervention and follow-up were in the predicted direction. However, they were not statistically significant.

On the subscales of the Classroom Observation Measure examining the effects of the EI program on problem behaviours for the entire sample, no intervention effects were found. There were differences in mean values over time between the EI group compared with the control cohort with the EI group showing some decreases in the symptoms of problem behaviour. However, these differences were not statistically significant at post-intervention or six-month follow-up.

Findings at the school level in terms of behaviour change in the EI group compared to the control cohort lend support to the hypothesis that the school component of the EI program would reduce the symptoms of problem behaviours in children. It must be noted, however, that the significant effect of reduced scores was only evident for the full sample at post-intervention on the SDQ (Teacher). The Classroom Observation measure reported no intervention effects. Therefore, these findings should be interpreted with caution.

Increase in Pro-social Behaviours. It was expected that there would be an intervention effect for the EI group in terms of an increase in pro-social behaviours in the school setting at post-intervention and follow-up compared with the control cohort. It was also predicted that effects would be greater for the indicated group compared with the full sample. Through the children's participation in the EI curriculum and through the teacher's management of the class group it was expected that there would be an increase in pro-social responses in the school setting. For the full sample, there were statistically significant differences found on the scores of the SDQ (Teacher) measuring pro-social responses compared with the control group at post-intervention and six-month follow-up. The reduction in pro-social mean scores from pre-intervention to six-month follow-up accounted for these differences in the EI full sample. The increase in pro-social behaviours within this cohort revealed an intervention effect that was sustained over time in comparison to the control group where no significant changes were apparent. On the SDQ (Teacher) measure of peer relationships there were differing mean score values between pre- and post-intervention indicating significant gains made for the EI cohort in comparison to the control group. However, this effect was no longer significant at the six-month follow-up period. On the SDQ (Teacher) measure of anxiety there were no statistically significant differences between mean values of the EI group compared with the control group between pre- and post-intervention. However, a significant increase in mean values scores was found in the EI sample at six-month follow-up compared with the control cohort.

For the EI indicated group, there were significant differences between this cohort and the control group indicated sample between pre- and post-intervention on the measures of pro-social behaviour and peer relationships. The findings from this second research question confirms that the school component of the EI program would increase the incidence of pro-social behaviours in children. However, the increases in mean values were only statistically significant for pro-social behaviours at six-month follow-up for the indicated sample of the EI group compared with the indicated control cohort.

Intervention Effects at the Home Level

Reduction in Aversive Parenting Strategies. In terms of the intervention effects of the home component of the EI program, it was predicted that there would be an intervention effect surrounding parents' employment of strategies to assist in the management of children's behaviours. It was predicted that parents participating in the parent training component of the EI program would report a decrease in the use of aversive parenting strategies and an increase in proactive strategies at post-intervention and six-month follow-up compared with those parents designated to control conditions. These predictions were based on the fifth research question. For the treatment sample there were no statistically significant differences on measures of parenting practices compared with the entire control cohort at post-intervention and six-month follow-up. In terms of the indicated sample there were no significant differences compared with the indicated control sample on parenting practices. Finally, there were no statistically significant differences in the use of parenting strategies within the universal sample of the EI group compared with the entire control cohort. Time effects were identified for the treatment, indicated and universal

84

samples of the EI group at post-intervention and six-month follow-up compared to the control group.

While time effects were identified across all groups, the above findings suggest that the home component of the EI program did not influence a change in parenting practices.

Reduction in Problem Behaviours. There was an expectation of a reduction in conduct problems in the home setting at post-intervention and follow-up for the full and indicated EI samples compared with the full and indicated samples of the control group. There was also an expectation that the effects for children in the indicated group would be greater in comparison to those included in the full sample. The author anticipated that, as a result of the parent's involvement in the parent training component of the program, parent competence in managing children's behaviour would be increased, which would in turn reduce the symptoms of problem behaviours in children at the home level. These predictions were centred on the third research question with results summarised as follows. There were no significant intervention effects on the core variables measuring conduct problems on the SDQ (Parent) at post-intervention compared to the control group for the full EI sample and the EI indicated group. However, there was a statistically significant effect for time evident in the full and indicated samples compared with the full and indicated control samples respectively. The extent of the differences in scores over time was accounted for by a reduction in mean values for the full and indicated sample of children in the EI group between pre- and post-intervention.

These findings suggest that the home component of the EI program failed to significantly reduce the symptoms of problem behaviours in children.

Increase in Pro-social Behaviours. Within the home setting, there was the expectation of an intervention effect for the EI group compared with the control group in terms of an increase in pro-social behaviours in the home setting at post-intervention and follow-up. Again, the prediction was held that the effects for the EI indicated group would be greater compared with those of the full EI sample. Through the parent's engagement in the parent training component of the program and the expected positive outcomes associated with this engagement it was predicted that there would be an increase in pro-social responses in children in the home setting.

The findings for the fourth research question are presented hereafter. For the full EI and indicated samples there were no intervention effects on the scores of the SDQ measuring pro-social responses compared with the control group at post-intervention and six-month follow-up. For the measure of peer relationships on the SDQ no intervention effects were found for either the full EI or indicated sample and for the measure of anxiety on the SDQ no intervention effects were identified for the full EI or indicated samples at post-intervention and sixth-month follow-up.

However, there was a main effect for time for the EI and control full and indicated samples. These outcomes would appear to indicate that the home component of the EI program failed to significantly increase pro-social responses in children.

Summary of Findings

The aim of the EI study was primarily to evaluate an early intervention and prevention program for children and families at-risk of conduct problems. Current advances in the scientific literature focussing on early intervention and prevention strategies to reduce the incidence of conduct problems in children and families identified that further research was necessary to determine the underlying variables associated with behaviour change at the school and home level. Existing models of treatment have targeted universal populations. However, the costs incurred in the delivery of such intervention frameworks make them unsustainable in regular community settings. Further, existing interventions require highly trained consultants as part of the implementation process, influencing parent, teacher and school administrators' reliance on such support. Finally, current frameworks target children on their entry into year one and fail to support children in the preschool year. This study sought to make a unique contribution to the existing body of knowledge by evaluating an early intervention program that was easily disseminable in regular school communities and that would target children on their entry into preschool.

The first aim of the EI study was to determine the social validity of the EI program as evidenced by teacher, parent and child engagement in the intervention. The evaluation revealed that, at the post-intervention period, teachers, parents and the behaviour consultant reported high levels of satisfaction with the EI program. The high rates of participation, retention and satisfaction give weight to this finding. Specifically, teacher, parent and consultant participants reported increased confidence

86

in managing problem behaviour in children at the post-intervention period. Further, teachers indicated that they had benefited from their involvement in the program as evidenced through their enthusiasm for the utility of the program design.

In terms of the second aim which sought to determine the effectiveness of the EI program as a means of reducing the incidence of problem behaviours in children at the home and school level, the findings of the study were mixed. At the school level an intervention effect was found at post-intervention with significant differences between the EI full cohort compared with the full control group. The findings of the SDQ (Teacher) reports indicate that there were some changes in the behaviour of children in the EI full sample. However, in terms of the findings of the classroom observation measure, no behaviour change was identified. The incongruity between the outcomes of the two teacher reports requires further discussion.

In terms of the findings from the SDQ (Teacher) report an explanation for the changes of behaviour in children, compared with the findings of the classroom observation measure may be attributed to a potential Hawthorne effect (Babbie, 1992). Teachers involved in the study were required to complete the SDQ (Teacher). For teachers assigned to experimental conditions, their completion of the SDQ (Teacher) may have been potentially compromised by a motivation to see changes in the behaviour in children as a result of the class' engagement in the program.

The home component of the Early Intervention program revealed no significant intervention effects at post-intervention or six-month follow-up. Based on current advances in preventative research it would seem that the design of the EI program home component should serve to reduce the risk of children developing problem behaviour. The reasons for the lack of significant reported change at the home level for the more at-risk children who engaged in the EI program are unclear. One possible explanation could be that the majority of parents of indicated children attended only one third of the parent training component of the program. This reduced dosage may have accounted for a lack of reported change in parenting practices. Further, limited changes in the parent's management of the child may have influenced the degree of behaviour change in the child in the home setting. Despite the findings of the EI study associated with the home component of the EI intervention, other early intervention and prevention studies targeting children and families at-risk have reported lower incidences in problem behaviours for intervention groups compared to control at the home level. Such outcomes lend support to the

87

significance of other intervention frameworks in reducing problem behaviours in children in the home setting. Programs identified in an earlier section of this book such as 'Head Start' (Webster-Stratton, 1998), 'First Step to Success' (Walker et al., 1998) and 'Fast Track' (Conduct Problems Prevention Research Group, 2002) support the effective influences of early intervention models on the family domain. Such findings reinforce the significance of evaluating the effects of early intervention frameworks to develop a more comprehensive understanding of the variables influencing effective implementation outcomes.

In terms of the EI Program investigation, the author's methodologies were significantly informed by existing intervention trials exploring multicomponent program designs. Outcome and process measures and procedures of participant recruitment and engagement included in the EI trial were considered within the framework of current advances in early intervention and prevention science. Despite the significant parallels between the methodologies of the EI trial and investigations such as Head Start, First Step to Success and Fast Track, there were significant differences in outcomes at the home level for the EI program. On all outcome measures for children at the home level there were small, but insignificant changes identified over time. As mentioned in an earlier section of this book, the limited participation and engagement in the parent training component of the program for the parents of those children identified as more at-risk for ongoing behaviour problems may have accounted for the lack of change in the behaviours of children compared with outcomes from similar studies. The participation rates for the home component of the Head Start, First Step to Success and Fast Track trials were high, and were instrumental in the facilitation of significant outcomes. A key strategy employed by all of the aforementioned trials to encourage high levels of engagement in the home component of each program involved regular payment of participants for their attendance. In one of the above studies researchers provided transport to and from the parent training venue for parents with limited financial support. These procedures served to encourage high levels of engagement and retention for parents participating in the research. While such strategies assisted in the recruitment of parents of at-risk children, financial constraints associated with the EI study did not allow for this approach to be adopted. Further, while the inclusion of financial incentives may serve to encourage greater participation within a sample of participants, there is some question regarding the sustainability of such an approach for schools and community groups most in need of early intervention and prevention programs.

Strengths and Limitations

There were a number of strengths in the EI Program evaluation that warrant discussion. First, the sample size for the investigation was large and the retention rate high. This enabled the author to collect sufficient data to permit the generalisability of findings to other community populations. Second, the socio-demographic composition of participating schools was homogenous, allowing for valid comparisons between school groups. Third, teachers, administrative staff and parents involved in the trial were extremely supportive of the intentions of the research, facilitating a cooperative dynamic conducive to the implementation of the program and collection of data. Fourth, teachers in the EI group were consistent in the delivery of the EI curriculum and related strategies of management. This ensured that the study maintained high treatment integrity and allowed for the examination of key variables associated with behaviour change. Clearly, the strengths of the trial lend support to the need for community based early intervention and prevention programs that offer assistance to schools and families in remediating the effects of problem behaviour in children at the home and school level.

There were a number of limitations of the EI study that were largely influenced by time and resource restraints that may have restricted the interpretation of findings. First, teachers were responsible for screening of children for inclusion in the trial, as well as completing outcome and treatment integrity measures. With respect to screening, although all teachers were thoroughly trained in the screening process, the absence of alternative processes to provide a more holistic approach to screening may have limited the recruitment process. Further, the teacher's involvement in screening children for inclusion in the study may have raised ethical concerns regarding the potential stigmatising effects associated with screening. However, the author attempted to address this concern by providing an extra series of outcome measures for teachers to complete that targeted a number of children representing a normative sample. These measures were included with the indicated cohort measures so as to conceal the identity of the originally identified at-risk group. In terms of teachers completing outcome measures on child behaviour at the school level, for those teachers in the EI cohort, there may have been a potential Hawthorne effect (Babbie,

1992) as a result of their engagement in the research. Teachers assigned to the intervention conditions may have developed a biased perspective concerning their perceptions of children's behaviour as a result of their desire to see the program successfully implemented in the school setting. Finally, teachers in the EI group were also responsible for the evaluation of treatment integrity. Using an additional treatment integrity measure to supplement the teacher's evaluation may have given weight to these conclusions.

Second, although the school component of the EI intervention led to positive gains, it cannot be assumed that behaviour change in children in the EI group can be attributed solely to the intervention's effects. Processes and mechanisms associated with the school component of the program accounting for change require further analysis to better understand factors influencing outcomes. Such in depth analysis was not possible given the current limitations of the study. However, the findings of the study do suggest that the school component of the EI program did serve to reduce the incidence of problem behaviours in children.

Third, the EI study was limited to follow-up data at the six-month follow-up period. To understand the effects of the EI program over time, longer-term follow-up (e.g. 2 years) to determine whether the intervention effects for the school component could be maintained is necessary.

Fourth, the emphasis of the school component on teacher management of child behaviour and the development of social skills in preschool aged children may have failed to adequately account for other psychosocial variables associated with the onset of dysfunction. Academic dysfunction, for example, which is known to contribute to the development of conduct problems in children (Coie et al., 1993), was not addressed in the EI program design. A significant challenge in early intervention and prevention research is how best to facilitate treatment programs that target the numerous factors influencing dysfunction in children and their families.

Fifth, there were a number of difficulties in encouraging families of children identified as more at-risk for ongoing conduct problems to engage in the home component of the EI intervention. Children with problem behaviour and their families usually struggle to access treatment. This trend may account for the limited gains reported in child behaviour at the home level for the study. The commitment to engaging in parent training can be demanding and so may influence lower parent engagement, in contrast to child-based interventions where engagement and attrition rates are better sustained. Clearly, alternative approaches to engage more at-risk parents in child management training are necessary to enhance treatment outcomes for children with conduct problems.

Recommendations

Implications for Future Research

Based on the presented findings of the EI study, including considerations of the strengths and limitations of the investigation, a number of recommendations can be made that serve to direct future research in early intervention and prevention for children and families at-risk of conduct problems. First, future treatment studies focussing on reducing the incidence of problem behaviours at the home and school level should give further exploration to factors beyond child management strategies and social skills training that may serve to arrest the development of conduct problems in children. The literature has identified a number of key variables that contribute to the development of problem behaviour in children. To better understand the interplay of factors that serve to arrest the child's trajectory towards dysfunction, further treatment studies must focus on the influences of such factors on behavioural outcomes.

Second, research in prevention must investigate alternative treatments to successfully engage more at-risk families. Low levels of engagement and high levels of attrition are common in preventative studies requiring active parent participation. Further research is necessary to determine the most efficient, cost effective and sustainable means by which such families can be targeted for treatment. Future investigations would be beneficial to assess those factors that influence parent selection and sustained engagement in treatment in order to build on existing intervention frameworks.

Third, further studies at the school level need to give consideration to the development of treatment programs that can be easily disseminated into regular school settings. Existing models of treatment are often costly and are overly reliant on the assistance of program consultants to implement and facilitate such interventions. Future investigations need to determine the efficacy of alternative school-based programs that can be readily implemented by regular school personnel to render them sustainable in regular community populations.

Fourth, future investigations into teachers' levels of expertise, experience and engagement with at-risk children and the class group as a moderator for behavioural outcomes in children are necessary. In order to more fully understand the influences of behaviour change at the school level, studies need to examine the potential influences of the teacher's training, experience and quality of engagement with children in managing problem behaviours in the classroom. Further research into teacher practices influencing behavioural responses in children may serve to assist in the development of school based treatments and teacher training programs designed to reduce the incidence and severity of conduct problems in child populations.

Finally, future directions in early intervention and prevention research should be directed towards the significance of home-school partnerships in assisting children at-risk of problem behaviour. Current research identifies the importance of treatment programs that encourage collaborative attempts between the home and school setting to impede the development of conduct problems in children. Further investigations need to be facilitated to determine the specific variables identified in the home and school setting that can be targeted in concert to influence positive behavioural outcomes in children and families at-risk of dysfunction.

Implications for Future Practice

The findings of the EI Program evaluation have also identified a number of recommendations to guide existing practice in the prevention of problem behaviour in children in regular community settings. First, appropriate screening procedures and treatment programs need to be developed that are more readily accessible to school communities in order to identify and effectively treat children more at-risk of conduct problems. Screening devices and intervention frameworks need to be cost effective and easily disseminable to ensure that they can be realistically implemented in regular school settings. Further, future screening approaches and intervention programs should be ethically and non-discriminatorily administered to reduce their potentially stigmatising effects.

Second, school administrators and teachers involved in the implementation of treatment programs should be adequately trained in the implementation and facilitation process. Professional supervision arrangements from suitably qualified personnel should be undertaken to ensure that programs are administered in a way that ensures the psychological health and well-being of children and their families.

Third, school personnel need to receive further training relating to the psychosocial variables surrounding dysfunctional behaviour in children. Many teachers working in regular classroom settings are ill-equipped to understand the significant influences underlying the at-risk child's behaviour both at the home and school level. As a result, teachers apply strategies that do not effectively address the needs of the child. Further, teachers should recognise the significance of developing effective partnerships with parents to work towards providing a more holistic approach to the management of children's behaviour that encompass variables in both the home and school setting.

Finally, existing community services targeting children and families at-risk of conduct problems require further evaluation to determine their social validity. Current models of treatment often fail to engage at-risk family groups, despite the attempts of clinicians and other professionals in the field to accommodate such families. Further, community and clinic based interventions need to facilitate more cooperative partnerships with schools in order to facilitate cogent intervention effects achieved through a more comprehensive treatment approach that targets the child and family at the home, school, and community level.

References

Achenbach, T.M., & Edelbrock, C.S. (1983). *Manual for the Child Behavior Checklist and Revised Child Behavior Profile.* Burlington, VT: University of Vermont.

Achenbach, T.M., & Edelbrock, C.S. (1986). *Manual for the Teacher's Report Form and Teacher Version of the Child Behavior Profile.* Burlington, VT: University of Vermont.

American Psychiatric Association. (2000). *The diagnostic and Statistical Manual of Mental Disorders* (4th ed., text rev.). Washington, DC: Author.

August, G.J., Egan, E.A., Realmuto, G.M., & Hektner, J.M. (2003). Parcelling component effects of a multifaceted prevention program for disruptive elementary school children. *Journal of Abnormal Child Psychology, 31 (5),* 515–527.

August, G.J., Realmuto, G.M., Hektner, J.M., & Bloomquist, M.L. (2001). An integrated components preventative intervention for aggressive elementary school children: The early risers program. *Journal of Consulting and Clinical Psychology, 69 (4),* 614–626.

Babbie, E.R. (2001). *The Practice of Social Research* (9th ed). California: Wadsworth, Inc.

Bates, J.E., Pettit, G.S., Dodge, K.A., & Ridge, B. (1998). Interaction of temperamental resistance to control and restrictive parenting in the development of externalising behavior. *Developmental Psychology, 34 (5),* 982-995.

Biglan, A., & Metzler, C.W. (in press). A public health perspective for research on family-focused interventions. In R.S. Ashery (Ed.), *Research Meeting on Drug Abuse Prevention Through Family Interventions.* Washington, DC: NIDA Research Monograph.

Bor, W., & Sanders, M.R. (2004). Correlates of self-reported coercive parenting of preschool-aged children at high risk for the development of conduct problems. *Australian and New Zealand Journal of Psychiatry, 38,* 738-745.

Brook, J.S., Whiteman, M., & Lu Zheng. (2002). Intergenerational transmission of risks for problem behavior. *Journal of Abnormal Child Psychology, 30 (1),* 65-76.

Bryk, A.S., Raudenbush, S.W., & Congdon, R.T. (2004). Hierarchical Linear and Non Linear Modelling (Version 6) [Computer software]. USA: Scientific Software International Inc.

Hollenstein, T., Granic, I., Stoolmiller, M., & Snyder, J. (2004). Rigidity in parent-child interactions and the development of externalizing and internalizing behaviour in early childhood. *Journal of Abnormal Child Psychology, 32, (6),* 595-608.

Hops, H., & Walker, H.M. (1988). *CLASS: Contingencies for Learning Academic and Social Skills.* Seattle, WA: Educational Achievement Systems.

Hovland, J., Smaby, M.H., & Maddux, C.D. (1996). At-risk children: Problems and interventions. *Elementary Guidance and Counselling, 31,* 43-50.

Huesmann, L.R., Eron, L.D., Lefkowitz, M.M., & Walder, L.O. (1984). Stability aggression over time and generations. *Developmental Psychology, 20,* 20-1134.

Jaffee, S.R., Caspi, A., Moffitt, T.E., Polo-Thomas, M., Price, T.S., & Taylor, (2004). The limits of child effects: Evidence for genetically mediated child effects corporal punishment but not on physical maltreatment. *Developmental Psychology, (6),* 1047-1058.

Jaffee, S.R., Caspi, A., Moffitt, T.E., & Taylor, A. (2004). Physical treatment victim to antisocial child: Evidence of an environmentally mediated cess. *Journal of Abnormal Psychology, 113, (1),* 44-55.

Johnson, S., Barrett, P.M., Dadds, M.R., Fox, T., & Shortt, A. (1999). The nostic interview schedule for children, adolescents, and parents: Initial reliability validity data. *Behavior Change, 16, (3),* 155-164.

Kastner, J.W. (1998). Clinical change in adolescent aggressive behavior: A p therapy approach. *Journal of Child and Adolescent Group Therapy, 8, (1),* 3.

Kazdin, A.E. (1996). Dropping out of child psychotherapy: Issues for research mplications for practice. *Clinical Child Psychology and Psychiatry, 1, (1),* 56.

Kazdin, A.E. (1995). Conduct disorders in childhood and adolescence. *opmental Clinical Psychology and Psychiatry, Vol 9.* London: Sage ations.

Kazdin, A.E. (1994). Models of dysfunction in developmental psychopathology. *l Psychology: Science and Practice, 1, (1),* 35-52.

azdin, A.E. (1993). Treatment of conduct disorder: Progress and directions in herapy research. *Development and Psychopathology, 5,* 277-310.

Caspi, A., Henry, B., McGee, R.O., Moffitt, T.E., & Silva, P.A. (1995). Temperamental origins of child and adolescent behavior problems: From age three to age fifteen, *Child Development, 66,* 55-68.

Caspi, A., McClay, J., Moffitt, T.E., & Mill, J. (2002). Role of genotype in the cycle of violence in maltreated children. *Science, 297,* 851-856.

Caspi, A., & Silva, P.A. (1995). Temperamental qualities at age three predict personality traits in young adulthood: Longitudinal evidence from a birth cohort. *Child Development, 66,* 486-498.

Cohen, J. (1992). Quantitative methods in psychology: a power primer. *Psychological Bulletin, 112 (1),* 155-159.

Coie, J.D., Watt, N.F., West, S.G., Hawkins, J.D., Asarnow, J.R., Markman, H.J., et al. (1993). The science of prevention: A conceptual framework and some directions for a national research program. *American Psychologist, 48 (10),* 1013-1022.

Conduct Problems Prevention Research Group (2002). Evaluation of the first 3 years of the fast track prevention trial with children at high risk for adolescent conduct problems. *Journal of Abnormal Child Psychology, 30 (1),* 19-35.

Conduct Problems Prevention Research Group (1999). Initial impact of the fast track prevention trial for conduct problems: 1. the high-risk sample. *Journal of Consulting and Clinical Psychology, 67 (5),* 631-647.

Cummings, E.M., Davies, P.T., & Campbell, S.B. (2000). *Developmental Psychopathology and the Family Process: Theory, Research and Clinical Implications.* New York: Guilford Press.

Dadds, M.R. (2002). An early intervention approach to children and families at-risk for psychopathology. In Terrance Patterson (Ed.), *Comprehensive Handbook of Psychotherapy, Vol. 2.* New York: John Wiley & Sons.

Dadds, M.R. (1995). Families, children, and the development of dysfunction. *Developmental Clinical Psychology and Psychiatry, Vol. 32,* London: Sage Publications.

Dadds, M.R., Maujean, A., & Fraser, J.A. (2003). Parenting and conduct problems in children: Australian data and psychometric properties of the Alabama parenting questionnaire. *Australian Psychologist, 38 (3),* 238–241.

Dadds, M., Spence, S.H., Holland, D.E., Barrett, P.M., & Laurens, K.R. (1997). Prevention and early intervention for anxiety disorders: a controlled trial. *Journal of Consulting and Clinical Psychology, 65 (4)*, 627-635.

Davis, C., Martin, G., Kosky, R., & O'Hanlon, A. (2000). *Early Intervention in the Mental Health of Young People.* Adelaide: Australian Early Intervention Network for Mental Health in Young People.

Dishion, T.J., McCord, J., & Poulin, F. (1999). When interventions harm: Peer groups and problem behaviour. *American Psychologist, 54 (9)*, 755-764.

Dishion, T.J., Nelson, S.E., Winter, C.E., & Bullock, B.M. (2004). Adolescent friendship as a dynamic system: Entropy and deviance in the etiology and course of male antisocial behavior. *Journal of Abnormal Child Psychology, 32 (6)*, 651-664.

Dodge, K.A., & Pettit, G.S. (2003). A biopsychosocial model of the development of chronic conduct problems in adolescence. *Developmental Psychology, 39*, 349-371.

Dupper, D.R., & Krishef, C.H. (1993). School-based social-cognitive skills training for middle school students with school behavior problems. *Children and Youth Services Review, 15*, 131-142.

Forehand, R., & McMahon, R.J. (1981). *Helping the Noncompliant Child: A Clinician's Guide to Parent Training.* New York: Guilford Press.

Frick, P.J. (2004). Developmental pathways to conduct disorder: Implications for serving youth who show severe aggressive and antisocial behaviour. *Psychology in the Schools, 41 (8)*, 823–834.

Frick, P.J. (2000). A comprehensive and individualised treatment approach for children and adolescents with conduct problems. *Cognitive and Behavioral Practice, 7*, 30-37.

Frick, P.J. (1998). *Conduct Disorders and Severe Antisocial Behavior.* New York: Plenum Press.

Frick, P.J., Cornell, A.H., Barry, C.T., Bodin, S.D., & Dane, H.E. (2003). Callous-unemotional traits and conduct problems in the prediction of conduct problem severity, aggression, and self-report of delinquency. *Journal of Abnormal Child Psychology, 31, (4)*, 457-470.

Frick, P.J., Cornell, A.H., Bodin, S.D., Dane, H.E., Barry, C.T., & Loney, B.R. (2003). Callous-unemotional traits and developmental pathways to severe conduct problems. *Developmental Psychology, 39, (2)*, 246-260.

Frick, P.J., & Loney, B.R. (2002) Understanding the associa and child antisocial behavior. In R.J. Mc Mahon, & R.D. Peters (*Parental Dysfunction on Children* (pp. 105–126). New York: Klu Academic/Plenum Publishers.

Frick, P.J., & Morris, A.S. (2004). Temperamental and dev to conduct problems. *Journal of Clinical Child and Adolescent* 54–68.

Greenberg, M.T., Domitrovich, C., & Bumbarger, B. (200 mental disorders in school-aged children: Current state of the f *Treatment, 4, (1)* 1-62.

Greenberg, M.T., Domitrovich, C., & Bumbarger, B. (1 *Disorders in School-Age Children: A Review of the Effectiver Programs.* USA: Pennsylvania State University.

Gresham, F.M., Lane, K.L., MacMillan, D.L., & Bocia and academic profiles of externalising and internalising grou emotional behavioral disorders. *Behavioral Disorders, 24, (*

Hartman, R.R., Stage, S.A., & Webster-Stratton, C. (. analysis of parent training outcomes: Examining the influe (inattention, impulsivity, and hyperactivity problems), par factors. *Journal of Child Psychology and Psychiatry, 44,*

Hawes, D.J., & Dadds, M.R. (2004). Australian data properties for the strengths and difficulties questionnaire *Zealand Journal of Psychiatry, 38*, 644–651.

Henggeler, S.W., Schoenwald, S.K., Borduin, C.M Cunningham, P.B. (1998). *Multisystemic Treatment of Children and Adolescents.* London: The Guilford Press

Henry, B., Caspi, A., Moffitt, T.E., & Silva, P.A. familial predictors of violent and non-violent criminal *Developmental Psychology, 32, (4)*, 614-623.

Hoff, K.E., & DuPaul, G.J. (1998). Reducing di education classrooms: The use of self-management s *Review, 27, (2)*, 290-303.

Kazdin, A.E. (1992). Overt and covert antisocial behavior: Child and family characteristics among psychiatric inpatient children. *Journal of Child and Family Studies, 1, (1),* 3-20.

Kazdin, A.E., Ayers, W.A., Bass, D., & Rogers, A. (1990). Empirical and clinical focus of child and adolescent psychotherapy research. *Journal of Consulting and Clinical Psychology, 58, (6),* 729-740.

Kazdin, A.E., & Esveldt-Dawson, K. (1986). The interview for antisocial behavior: Psychometric characteristics and concurrent validity with child psychiatric inpatients. *Journal of Psychopathology and Behavioral Assessment, 8,* 289-303.

Kazdin, A.E., Holland, L., & Crowley, M. (1997). Family experience of barriers to treatment and premature termination from child therapy. *Journal of Consulting and Clinical Psychology, 65, (3),* 453–463.

Kazdin, A.E., & Kagan, J. (1994). Models of dysfunction in developmental psychopathology. *Clinical Psychology: Science and Practice, 1, (1),* 35-52.

Kazdin, A.E., Siegel, T.C., & Bass, D. (1992). Cognitive problem-solving skills training and parent management training in the treatment of antisocial behavior in children. *Journal of Consulting and Clinical Psychology, 60, (5),* 733-747.

Kazdin, A.E., & Weisz, J.R. (1998). Identifying and developing empirically supported child and adolescent treatments. *Journal of Consulting and Clinical Psychology, 66, (1),* 19-36.

Keiley, M.K., Bates, J.E., Dodge, K.A. & Pettit, G.S. (2000). A cross-domain growth analysis: Externalizing and internalizing behaviours during 8 years of childhood. *Journal of Abnormal Child Psychology, 28, (2),* 161-179.

Kendall, P.C. (1993). Cognitive-behavioral therapies with youth: Guiding theory, current status, and emerging developments. *Journal of Counselling and Clinical Psychology, 61, (2),* 235-247.

Kendall, P.C., & Panichelli-Mindel, S.M. (1995). Cognitive-behavioral treatments. *Journal of Abnormal Child Psychology, 23, (1),* 107-124.

Knitzer, J. (1985). Mental health services to children. *Journal of Clinical Child Psychology, 14,* 178-251.

Kratzer, L., & Hodgins, S. (1997). Adult outcomes of child conduct problems: A cohort study. *Journal of Abnormal Child Psychology, 25,* 65–81.

Lahey, B.B., Loeber, R., Quay, H.C., Frick, P.J., Applegate, B., Zhang, Q., et al. (1995). Four-year longitudinal study of conduct disorder in boys: Patterns of predictors of persistence. *Journal of Abnormal Psychology, 104,* 83–93.

Laird, R.D., Jordan, K.Y., Dodge, K.A., Pettit, G.S., & Bates, J.E. (2001). Peer rejection in childhood, involvement with antisocial peers in early adolescence, and the development of externalising behavior problems. *Development and Psychopathology, 13,* 337-354.

Larmar, S.A. (2002). *Encouraging Positive Behaviour in the Classroom.* Unpublished Manual.

Larmar, S.A. (2002). *Encouraging Positive Behaviour in Young Children.* Unpublished Manual.

Larmar, S.A. (2002). *The Early Impact Program: A Program for Encouraging Positive Behaviour in Young Children.* Unpublished Manual.

Larmar, S.A., & Dadds, M.R. (2002). *Behaviour Consultant Report Form.* Unpublished Measure.

Larmar, S.A., & Dadds, M.R. (2002). *Classroom Observation Schedule.* Unpublished Measure.

Larmar, S.A., & Dadds, M.R. (2002). *Parent Self-Report.* Unpublished Measure.

Larmar, S.A., & Dadds, M.R. (2002). *Peer Nomination Interview Schedule.* Unpublished Measure.

Larmar, S.A., & Dadds, M.R. (2002). *Teacher Self-Report.* Unpublished Measure.

Little, E., & Hudson, A. (1998). Conduct problems and treatment across home and school: A review of the literature. *Behavior Change, 15, (4),* 213-227.

Lochman, J.E., & Wells, K.C. (1996). *Preventing Childhood Disorders, Substance Abuse, and Delinquency.* London: Sage Publications.

Loeber, R. (1988). The natural histories of juvenile conduct problems, substance use and delinquency: Evidence for developmental progressions. In B.B. Lahey & A.E. Kazdin (Eds.), *Advances in Clinical Child Psychology, Vol. 11,* pp. 73-124. New York: Plenum Press.

Loeber, R., Drinkwater, M., Yin, Y., & Anderson, S.J. (2000). Stability of family interaction from ages 6 to 18. *Journal of Abnormal Child Psychology, 28, (4),* 353-369.

Loeber, R., & Farrington, D.P. (2000). Young children who commit crime: Epidemiology, developmental origins, risk factors, early interventions, and policy implications. *Development and Psychopathology, 12,* 737-762.

Loeber, R., Farrington, D.P., Stouthhamer-Loeber, M., Moffitt, T.E., Caspi, A., & Lynam, D. (2001). Male mental health problems, psychopathy, and personality traits: Key findings from the first 14 years of the Pittsburgh youth study. *Clinical Child and Family Psychology Review, 4, (4),* 273-297.

Loeber, R., Farrington, D.P., Stouthhamer-Loeber, M., & Van Kammen, W.B. (1998). *Antisocial Behavior and Mental Health Problems: Explanatory Factors in Childhood and Adolescence.* Mahwah, NJ: Lawrence Erlbaum.

Loeber, R., Green, S.M., Lahey, B.B., Frick, P.J., & McBurnett, K. (2000). Findings on disruptive behavior disorders from the first decade of the developmental trends study. *Clinical Child and Family Psychology Review, 3, (1),* 37–60.

Loeber, R., Lahey, B.B., & Thomas, C. (1991). Diagnostic conundrum of oppositional defiant disorder and conduct disorder. *Journal of Abnormal Psychology, 100, (3),* 379–390.

Loeber, R., Wung, P., Keenan, K., Giroux, B., Stouthamer-Loeber, M., Van Kammen, W.B., & Maughan, B. (1993). Developmental pathways in disruptive child behavior. *Development and Psychopathology, 5,* 103-133.

McCord, J., Tremblay, R.E., Vitaro, F., & Desmarais-Gervais, L. (1994). 'Boys' disruptive behavior, school adjustment and delinquency: The montreal prevention experiment. *International Journal of Behavioral Development, (17),* 739-752.

McMahon, R.J., & Wells, K.C. (1989). *Treatment of Childhood Disorders.* New York: The Guilford Press.

Moffitt, T.E. (1993). Adolescence-limited and life-course-persistent antisocial behavior: A developmental taxonomy. *Psychological Review, 100, (4),* 674-701.

Moffitt, T.E., & Caspi, A. (2001). Childhood predictors differentiate life-course persistent and adolescent limited pathways among males and females. *Development and Psychopathology, 13,* 355-375.

Offord, D., Boyle, M.H., Racine, Y.A., Fleming, J.E., Cadman, D.T., Blum, H.M., et al. (1992). Outcome, prognosis, and risk in a longitudinal follow-up study. *Journal of the American Academy of Child and Adolescent Psychiatry. 31*, 916-923.

Olsen, S.L., Bates, J.E., Sandy, J.M., & Lanthier, R. (2000). Early developmental precursors of externalising behavior in middle childhood and adolescence. *Journal of Abnormal Child Psychology, 28, (2),* 119-133.

Patterson, G.R., DeBaryshe, B.D., & Ramsey, E. (1989). A developmental perspective on antisocial behaviour. *American Psychologist, 44, (2),* 329-335.

Patterson, G.R., DeGarmo, D.S., & Forgatch, M.S. (2004). Systemic changes in families following prevention trials. *Journal of Abnormal Child Psychology. 32, (6),* 621-634.

Patterson, G.R., DeGarmo, D.S., & Knutson, N. (2000). Hyperactive and antisocial behavior: Comorbid or two points in the same process. *Development and Psychopathology, 12,* 91-106.

Prinz, R.J., & Miller, G.E. (1996). *Preventing Childhood Disorders, Substance Abuse, and Delinquency.* London: Sage Publications.

Prinz, R.J., & Miller, G.E. (1994). Family-based treatment for childhood antisocial behavior: Experimental influences on dropout and engagement. *Journal of Consulting and Clinical Psychology, 62, (3),* 645–650.

Raudenbush, S.W., & Bryk, A.S. (2002). *Hierarchical Linear Models: Applications and Data Analysis Methods.* (2nd ed). London: Sage Publications.

Raine, A. (2002). Biosocial studies of antisocial and violent behavior in children and adults: A review. *Journal of Abnormal Child Psychology, 30,* 311-326.

Reid, J.B., Eddy, J.M., Fetrow, R.A., & Stoolmiller, M. (1999). Description and immediate impacts of a preventative intervention for conduct problems. *American Journal of Community Psychology, 27,* 483-509.

Reitsma-Street, M., Offord, D.R., & Finch, T. (1985). Pairs of same-sexed siblings discordant for antisocial behavior. *British Journal of Psychology, 146,* 415-423.

Rutter, M. (1989). Pathways from childhood to adult life. *Journal of Child Psychology and Psychiatry, 30,* 23-51.

Rutter, M., Maughan, B., Mortimore, P., & Ouston, J. (1979). *Fifteen Thousand Hours: Secondary Schools and Their Effects on Children.* London: Open Books Publishing.

Caspi, A., Henry, B., McGee, R.O., Moffitt, T.E., & Silva, P.A. (1995). Temperamental origins of child and adolescent behavior problems: From age three to age fifteen, *Child Development, 66,* 55-68.

Caspi, A., McClay, J., Moffitt, T.E., & Mill, J. (2002). Role of genotype in the cycle of violence in maltreated children. *Science, 297,* 851-856.

Caspi, A., & Silva, P.A. (1995). Temperamental qualities at age three predict personality traits in young adulthood: Longitudinal evidence from a birth cohort. *Child Development, 66,* 486-498.

Cohen, J. (1992). Quantitative methods in psychology: a power primer. *Psychological Bulletin, 112 (1),* 155-159.

Coie, J.D., Watt, N.F., West, S.G., Hawkins, J.D., Asarnow, J.R., Markman, H.J., et al. (1993). The science of prevention: A conceptual framework and some directions for a national research program. *American Psychologist, 48 (10),* 1013-1022.

Conduct Problems Prevention Research Group (2002). Evaluation of the first 3 years of the fast track prevention trial with children at high risk for adolescent conduct problems. *Journal of Abnormal Child Psychology, 30 (1),* 19-35.

Conduct Problems Prevention Research Group (1999). Initial impact of the fast track prevention trial for conduct problems: 1. the high-risk sample. *Journal of Consulting and Clinical Psychology, 67 (5),* 631-647.

Cummings, E.M., Davies, P.T., & Campbell, S.B. (2000). *Developmental Psychopathology and the Family Process: Theory, Research and Clinical Implications.* New York: Guilford Press.

Dadds, M.R. (2002). An early intervention approach to children and families at-risk for psychopathology. In Terrance Patterson (Ed.), *Comprehensive Handbook of Psychotherapy, Vol. 2.* New York: John Wiley & Sons.

Dadds, M.R. (1995). Families, children, and the development of dysfunction. *Developmental Clinical Psychology and Psychiatry, Vol. 32,* London: Sage Publications.

Dadds, M.R., Maujean, A., & Fraser, J.A. (2003). Parenting and conduct problems in children: Australian data and psychometric properties of the Alabama parenting questionnaire. *Australian Psychologist, 38 (3),* 238–241.

Dadds, M., Spence, S.H., Holland, D.E., Barrett, P.M., & Laurens, K.R. (1997). Prevention and early intervention for anxiety disorders: a controlled trial. *Journal of Consulting and Clinical Psychology, 65 (4),* 627-635.

Davis, C., Martin, G., Kosky, R., & O'Hanlon, A. (2000). *Early Intervention in the Mental Health of Young People.* Adelaide: Australian Early Intervention Network for Mental Health in Young People.

Dishion, T.J., McCord, J., & Poulin, F. (1999). When interventions harm: Peer groups and problem behaviour. *American Psychologist, 54 (9),* 755-764.

Dishion, T.J., Nelson, S.E., Winter, C.E., & Bullock, B.M. (2004). Adolescent friendship as a dynamic system: Entropy and deviance in the etiology and course of male antisocial behavior. *Journal of Abnormal Child Psychology, 32 (6),* 651-664.

Dodge, K.A., & Pettit, G.S. (2003). A biopsychosocial model of the development of chronic conduct problems in adolescence. *Developmental Psychology, 39,* 349-371.

Dupper, D.R., & Krishef, C.H. (1993). School-based social-cognitive skills training for middle school students with school behavior problems. *Children and Youth Services Review, 15,* 131-142.

Forehand, R., & McMahon, R.J. (1981). *Helping the Noncompliant Child: A Clinician's Guide to Parent Training.* New York: Guilford Press.

Frick, P.J. (2004). Developmental pathways to conduct disorder: Implications for serving youth who show severe aggressive and antisocial behaviour. *Psychology in the Schools, 41 (8),* 823–834.

Frick, P.J. (2000). A comprehensive and individualised treatment approach for children and adolescents with conduct problems. *Cognitive and Behavioral Practice, 7,* 30-37.

Frick, P.J. (1998). *Conduct Disorders and Severe Antisocial Behavior.* New York: Plenum Press.

Frick, P.J., Cornell, A.H., Barry, C.T., Bodin, S.D., & Dane, H.E. (2003). Callous-unemotional traits and conduct problems in the prediction of conduct problem severity, aggression, and self-report of delinquency. *Journal of Abnormal Child Psychology, 31, (4),* 457-470.

Frick, P.J., Cornell, A.H., Bodin, S.D., Dane, H.E., Barry, C.T., & Loney, B.R. (2003). Callous-unemotional traits and developmental pathways to severe conduct problems. *Developmental Psychology, 39, (2),* 246-260.

Frick, P.J., & Loney, B.R. (2002) Understanding the association between parent and child antisocial behavior. In R.J. Mc Mahon, & R.D. Peters (Eds.), *The Effects of Parental Dysfunction on Children* (pp. 105–126). New York: Kluwer Academic/Plenum Publishers.

Frick, P.J., & Morris, A.S. (2004). Temperamental and developmental pathways to conduct problems. *Journal of Clinical Child and Adolescent Psychology, 33, (1),* 54–68.

Greenberg, M.T., Domitrovich, C., & Bumbarger, B. (2001). The prevention of mental disorders in school-aged children: Current state of the field. *Prevention and Treatment, 4, (1)* 1-62.

Greenberg, M.T., Domitrovich, C., & Bumbarger, B. (1999). *Preventing Mental Disorders in School-Age Children: A Review of the Effectiveness of Prevention Programs.* USA: Pennsylvania State University.

Gresham, F.M., Lane, K.L., MacMillan, D.L., & Bocian, K.M. (1999). Social and academic profiles of externalising and internalising groups: Risk factors for emotional behavioral disorders. *Behavioral Disorders, 24, (3),* 231–245.

Hartman, R.R., Stage, S.A., & Webster-Stratton, C. (2003). A growth curve analysis of parent training outcomes: Examining the influence of child risk factors (inattention, impulsivity, and hyperactivity problems), parental and family risk factors. *Journal of Child Psychology and Psychiatry, 44, (3),* 388-398.

Hawes, D.J., & Dadds, M.R. (2004). Australian data and psychometric properties for the strengths and difficulties questionnaire. *Australian and New Zealand Journal of Psychiatry, 38,* 644–651.

Henggeler, S.W., Schoenwald, S.K., Borduin, C.M., Rowland, M.D., & Cunningham, P.B. (1998). *Multisystemic Treatment of Antisocial Behavior in Children and Adolescents.* London: The Guilford Press.

Henry, B., Caspi, A., Moffitt, T.E., & Silva, P.A. (1996). Temperamental and familial predictors of violent and non-violent criminal convictions: Age 3 to age 18. *Developmental Psychology, 32, (4),* 614-623.

Hoff, K.E., & DuPaul, G.J. (1998). Reducing disruptive behavior in general education classrooms: The use of self-management strategies. *School Psychology Review, 27, (2),* 290-303.

Hollenstein, T., Granic, I., Stoolmiller, M., & Snyder, J. (2004). Rigidity in parent-child interactions and the development of externalizing and internalizing behaviour in early childhood. *Journal of Abnormal Child Psychology, 32, (6),* 595-608.

Hops, H., & Walker, H.M. (1988). *CLASS: Contingencies for Learning Academic and Social Skills.* Seattle, WA: Educational Achievement Systems.

Hovland, J., Smaby, M.H., & Maddux, C.D. (1996). At-risk children: Problems and interventions. *Elementary Guidance and Counselling, 31,* 43-50.

Huesmann, L.R., Eron, L.D., Lefkowitz, M.M., & Walder, L.O. (1984). Stability of aggression over time and generations. *Developmental Psychology, 20,* 1120–1134.

Jaffee, S.R., Caspi, A., Moffitt, T.E., Polo-Thomas, M., Price, T.S., & Taylor, A. (2004). The limits of child effects: Evidence for genetically mediated child effects on corporal punishment but not on physical maltreatment. *Developmental Psychology, 40, (6),* 1047-1058.

Jaffee, S.R., Caspi, A., Moffitt, T.E., & Taylor, A. (2004). Physical maltreatment victim to antisocial child: Evidence of an environmentally mediated process. *Journal of Abnormal Psychology, 113, (1),* 44-55.

Johnson, S., Barrett, P.M., Dadds, M.R., Fox, T., & Shortt, A. (1999). The diagnostic interview schedule for children, adolescents, and parents: Initial reliability and validity data. *Behavior Change, 16, (3),* 155–164.

Kastner, J.W. (1998). Clinical change in adolescent aggressive behavior: A group therapy approach. *Journal of Child and Adolescent Group Therapy, 8, (1),* 23-33.

Kazdin, A.E. (1996). Dropping out of child psychotherapy: Issues for research and implications for practice. *Clinical Child Psychology and Psychiatry, 1, (1),* 133–156.

Kazdin, A.E. (1995). Conduct disorders in childhood and adolescence. *Developmental Clinical Psychology and Psychiatry, Vol 9.* London: Sage Publications.

Kazdin, A.E. (1994). Models of dysfunction in developmental psychopathology. *Clinical Psychology: Science and Practice, 1, (1),* 35-52.

Kazdin, A.E. (1993). Treatment of conduct disorder: Progress and directions in psychotherapy research. *Development and Psychopathology, 5,* 277-310.

Kazdin, A.E. (1992). Overt and covert antisocial behavior: Child and family characteristics among psychiatric inpatient children. *Journal of Child and Family Studies, 1, (1),* 3-20.

Kazdin, A.E., Ayers, W.A., Bass, D., & Rogers, A. (1990). Empirical and clinical focus of child and adolescent psychotherapy research. *Journal of Consulting and Clinical Psychology, 58, (6),* 729-740.

Kazdin, A.E., & Esveldt-Dawson, K. (1986). The interview for antisocial behavior: Psychometric characteristics and concurrent validity with child psychiatric inpatients. *Journal of Psychopathology and Behavioral Assessment, 8,* 289-303.

Kazdin, A.E., Holland, L., & Crowley, M. (1997). Family experience of barriers to treatment and premature termination from child therapy. *Journal of Consulting and Clinical Psychology, 65, (3),* 453–463.

Kazdin, A.E., & Kagan, J. (1994). Models of dysfunction in developmental psychopathology. *Clinical Psychology: Science and Practice, 1, (1),* 35-52.

Kazdin, A.E., Siegel, T.C., & Bass, D. (1992). Cognitive problem-solving skills training and parent management training in the treatment of antisocial behavior in children. *Journal of Consulting and Clinical Psychology, 60, (5),* 733-747.

Kazdin, A.E., & Weisz, J.R. (1998). Identifying and developing empirically supported child and adolescent treatments. *Journal of Consulting and Clinical Psychology, 66, (1),* 19-36.

Keiley, M.K., Bates, J.E., Dodge, K.A. & Pettit, G.S. (2000). A cross-domain growth analysis: Externalizing and internalizing behaviours during 8 years of childhood. *Journal of Abnormal Child Psychology, 28, (2),* 161-179.

Kendall, P.C. (1993). Cognitive-behavioral therapies with youth: Guiding theory, current status, and emerging developments. *Journal of Counselling and Clinical Psychology, 61, (2),* 235-247.

Kendall, P.C., & Panichelli-Mindel, S.M. (1995). Cognitive-behavioral treatments. *Journal of Abnormal Child Psychology, 23, (1),* 107-124.

Knitzer, J. (1985). Mental health services to children. *Journal of Clinical Child Psychology, 14,* 178-251.

Kratzer, L., & Hodgins, S. (1997). Adult outcomes of child conduct problems: A cohort study. *Journal of Abnormal Child Psychology, 25,* 65–81.

Lahey, B.B., Loeber, R., Quay, H.C., Frick, P.J., Applegate, B., Zhang, Q., et al. (1995). Four-year longitudinal study of conduct disorder in boys: Patterns of predictors of persistence. *Journal of Abnormal Psychology, 104,* 83–93.

Laird, R.D., Jordan, K.Y., Dodge, K.A., Pettit, G.S., & Bates, J.E. (2001). Peer rejection in childhood, involvement with antisocial peers in early adolescence, and the development of externalising behavior problems. *Development and Psychopathology, 13,* 337-354.

Larmar, S.A. (2002). *Encouraging Positive Behaviour in the Classroom.* Unpublished Manual.

Larmar, S.A. (2002). *Encouraging Positive Behaviour in Young Children.* Unpublished Manual.

Larmar, S.A. (2002). *The Early Impact Program: A Program for Encouraging Positive Behaviour in Young Children.* Unpublished Manual.

Larmar, S.A., & Dadds, M.R. (2002). *Behaviour Consultant Report Form.* Unpublished Measure.

Larmar, S.A., & Dadds, M.R. (2002). *Classroom Observation Schedule.* Unpublished Measure.

Larmar, S.A., & Dadds, M.R. (2002). *Parent Self-Report.* Unpublished Measure.

Larmar, S.A., & Dadds, M.R. (2002). *Peer Nomination Interview Schedule.* Unpublished Measure.

Larmar, S.A., & Dadds, M.R. (2002). *Teacher Self-Report.* Unpublished Measure.

Little, E., & Hudson, A. (1998). Conduct problems and treatment across home and school: A review of the literature. *Behavior Change, 15, (4),* 213-227.

Lochman, J.E., & Wells, K.C. (1996). *Preventing Childhood Disorders, Substance Abuse, and Delinquency.* London: Sage Publications.

Loeber, R. (1988). The natural histories of juvenile conduct problems, substance use and delinquency: Evidence for developmental progressions. In B.B. Lahey & A.E. Kazdin (Eds.), *Advances in Clinical Child Psychology, Vol. 11,* pp. 73-124. New York: Plenum Press.

Loeber, R., Drinkwater, M., Yin, Y., & Anderson, S.J. (2000). Stability of family interaction from ages 6 to 18. *Journal of Abnormal Child Psychology, 28, (4),* 353-369.

Loeber, R., & Farrington, D.P. (2000). Young children who commit crime: Epidemiology, developmental origins, risk factors, early interventions, and policy implications. *Development and Psychopathology, 12,* 737-762.

Loeber, R., Farrington, D.P., Stouthhamer-Loeber, M., Moffitt, T.E., Caspi, A., & Lynam, D. (2001). Male mental health problems, psychopathy, and personality traits: Key findings from the first 14 years of the Pittsburgh youth study. *Clinical Child and Family Psychology Review, 4, (4),* 273-297.

Loeber, R., Farrington, D.P., Stouthhamer-Loeber, M., & Van Kammen, W.B. (1998). *Antisocial Behavior and Mental Health Problems: Explanatory Factors in Childhood and Adolescence.* Mahwah, NJ: Lawrence Erlbaum.

Loeber, R., Green, S.M., Lahey, B.B., Frick, P.J., & McBurnett, K. (2000). Findings on disruptive behavior disorders from the first decade of the developmental trends study. *Clinical Child and Family Psychology Review, 3, (1),* 37–60.

Loeber, R., Lahey, B.B., & Thomas, C. (1991). Diagnostic conundrum of oppositional defiant disorder and conduct disorder. *Journal of Abnormal Psychology, 100, (3),* 379–390.

Loeber, R., Wung, P., Keenan, K., Giroux, B., Stouthamer-Loeber, M., Van Kammen, W.B., & Maughan, B. (1993). Developmental pathways in disruptive child behavior. *Development and Psychopathology, 5,* 103-133.

McCord, J., Tremblay, R.E., Vitaro, F., & Desmarais-Gervais, L. (1994). 'Boys' disruptive behavior, school adjustment and delinquency: The montreal prevention experiment. *International Journal of Behavioral Development, (17),* 739-752.

McMahon, R.J., & Wells, K.C. (1989). *Treatment of Childhood Disorders.* New York: The Guilford Press.

Moffitt, T.E. (1993). Adolescence-limited and life-course-persistent antisocial behavior: A developmental taxonomy. *Psychological Review, 100, (4),* 674-701.

Moffitt, T.E., & Caspi, A. (2001). Childhood predictors differentiate life-course persistent and adolescent limited pathways among males and females. *Development and Psychopathology, 13,* 355-375.

Offord, D., Boyle, M.H., Racine, Y.A., Fleming, J.E., Cadman, D.T., Blum, H.M., et al. (1992). Outcome, prognosis, and risk in a longitudinal follow-up study. *Journal of the American Academy of Child and Adolescent Psychiatry. 31*, 916-923.

Olsen, S.L., Bates, J.E., Sandy, J.M., & Lanthier, R. (2000). Early developmental precursors of externalising behavior in middle childhood and adolescence. *Journal of Abnormal Child Psychology, 28, (2)*, 119-133.

Patterson, G.R., DeBaryshe, B.D., & Ramsey, E. (1989). A developmental perspective on antisocial behaviour. *American Psychologist, 44, (2)*, 329-335.

Patterson, G.R., DeGarmo, D.S., & Forgatch, M.S. (2004). Systemic changes in families following prevention trials. *Journal of Abnormal Child Psychology. 32, (6)*, 621-634.

Patterson, G.R., DeGarmo, D.S., & Knutson, N. (2000). Hyperactive and antisocial behavior: Comorbid or two points in the same process. *Development and Psychopathology, 12*, 91-106.

Prinz, R.J., & Miller, G.E. (1996). *Preventing Childhood Disorders, Substance Abuse, and Delinquency.* London: Sage Publications.

Prinz, R.J., & Miller, G.E. (1994). Family-based treatment for childhood antisocial behavior: Experimental influences on dropout and engagement. *Journal of Consulting and Clinical Psychology, 62, (3)*, 645–650.

Raudenbush, S.W., & Bryk, A.S. (2002). *Hierarchical Linear Models: Applications and Data Analysis Methods.* (2nd ed). London: Sage Publications.

Raine, A. (2002). Biosocial studies of antisocial and violent behavior in children and adults: A review. *Journal of Abnormal Child Psychology, 30*, 311-326.

Reid, J.B., Eddy, J.M., Fetrow, R.A., & Stoolmiller, M. (1999). Description and immediate impacts of a preventative intervention for conduct problems. *American Journal of Community Psychology, 27*, 483-509.

Reitsma-Street, M., Offord, D.R., & Finch, T. (1985). Pairs of same-sexed siblings discordant for antisocial behavior. *British Journal of Psychology, 146*, 415-423.

Rutter, M. (1989). Pathways from childhood to adult life. *Journal of Child Psychology and Psychiatry, 30*, 23-51.

Rutter, M., Maughan, B., Mortimore, P., & Ouston, J. (1979). *Fifteen Thousand Hours: Secondary Schools and Their Effects on Children.* London: Open Books Publishing.

Sanders, M.R. (1999). Triple p-positive parenting program: Towards an empirically validated multilevel parenting and family support strategy for the prevention of behavior and emotional problems in children. *Clinical Child and Family Psychology Review, 2, (2),* 71-91.

Sanders, M.R., Gooley, S., & Nicholsen, J. (2000). Early intervention in conduct problems in children. Vol. 3. In: R. Kosky, A. O'Hanlon, G. Martin, & C. Davis (Eds.), *Clinical Approaches to Early Intervention in Child and Adolescent Mental Health, Vol. 3.* Adelaide: Australian Early Intervention Network for Mental Health in Young People.

Sanders, M.R., Tully, L.A., Baade, P.D., Lynch, M.E., Heywood, A.H., Pollard, G.E., & Youlden, D.R. (1999). A survey of parenting practices in Queensland: Implications for mental health promotion. *Health Promotion Journal of Australia, 9,(2),* 105-114.

Shaw, D.S., Owens, E.B., Vondra, J.I., Kennan, K., & Winslow, E.B. (1996). Early risk factors and pathways in the development of early disruptive behavior problems. *Development and Psychopathology. 8,* 679–699.

Shaw, D.S., Winslow, E.B., Owens, E.B., & Vondra, J.I. (1998). The development of early externalising problems among children from low-income families: A transformational perspective. *Journal of Abnormal Child Psychology, 26, (2),* 95-107.

Shelton, K.K., Frick, P.J., & Wooton, J. (1996). Assessment of parenting practices in families of elementary school-age children. *Journal of Clinical Child Psychology, 25,* 317-329.

Shelton, T.L., Barkley, R.A., Crosswait, C., Moorehouse, M., Fletcher, K., Barrett, S., Jenkins, L., & Metevia, L. (2000). Multimethod psychoeducational intervention for preschool children with disruptive behavior: Two-year post-treatment follow-up. *Journal of Abnormal Child Psychology, 28, (3),* 253–266.

Shochet, I.M., Dadds, M., Holland, D., Whitefield, K., Harnett, P.H., & Osgarby, S.M. (2001). The efficacy of a universal school-based program to prevent adolescent depression. *Journal of Clinical Child Psychology, 30, (3),* 303-315.

Silburn, S.R., Zubrick, S.R., Garton, A., Gurrin, L., Burton, P., Dalby, R., et al. (1996). *Western Australian Child Health Survey: Family and Community Health.* Pert, Western Australia: Australian Bureau of Statistics and the TVW Telethon Institute for Child Health Research.

Snyder, J., Prichard, J., Schrepferman, L., Patrick, M.R., & Stoolmiller, M. (2004). Child impulsiveness-inattention, early peer experiences, and the development of early onset conduct problems. *Journal of Abnormal Child Psychology, 32, (6),* 579-595.

Soodak, L.C., & Podell, D.M. (1994). Teachers' thinking about difficult-to-teach students. *Journal of Educational Research, 88, (1),* 44-51.

Spoth, R., Goldberg, C., & Redmond, C. (1999). Engaging families in longitudinal preventative intervention research: Discrete-time survival analysis of socio-economic and social-emotional risk factors. *Journal of Consulting and Clinical Psychology. 67, (1),* 157–163.

Spoth, R., Redmond, C., Hockaday, C., & Yeol Shin, C. (1996). Barriers to participation in family skills preventive interventions and their evaluations: A replication and extension. *Family Relations. 45, (3),* 247–254.

Tuma, J.M. (1989). Mental health services for children: The state of the art. *American Psychologist, 44,* 188-198.

Vitaro, F., Brendgen, M., Pagani, L., Tremblay, R.E., & Mc Duff, P. (1999). Disruptive behavior, peer association, and conduct disorder: Testing the developmental links through early intervention. *Development and Psychopathology, 11,* 287–304.

Walker, H.M., Kavanagh,K., Stiller, B., & Golly, A. (1998). First step to success: An early intervention approach to preventing school antisocial behavior. *Journal of Emotional and Behavioral Disorders, 6, (2),* 66–84.

Walker, H.M., Severson, H.H., Feil, E.G., Stiller, B., & Golly, A. (1998). First step to success: Intervening at the point of school entry to prevent antisocial behavior patterns. *Psychology in the Schools, 35, (3),* 259-269.

Waugh, A., & Forlin, C. (1998). "I really like the way you…" training parents to shape the behaviour of a-d/hd children: Is it effective? *Australian Journal of Guidance and Counselling, 8, (1),* 113-122.

Webster-Stratton, C. (1998). Preventing conduct problems in head start children: Strengthening parenting competencies. *Journal of Consulting and Clinical Psychology, 66, (5),* 715-730.

Webster-Stratton, C., & Hammond, M. (1998). Conduct problems and level of social competence in head start children: Prevalence, pervasiveness, and associated risk factors. *Clinical Child and Family Psychology Review, 1,* 101-124.

Webster-Stratton, C., Reid, M.J., & Baydar, N. (2004). Halting the development of conduct problems in head start children: The effects of parent training. *Journal of Clinical Child and Adolescent Psychology, 33, (2),* 279-291.

Webster-Stratton, C., Reid, M.J., & Hammond, M. (2001). Social skills and problem-solving training for children with early-onset conduct problems: Who benefits. *Journal of Child Psychology and Psychiatry, 42, (7),* 943-952.

STAGE ONE SCREENING MEASURE

CLASS TEACHER:_____
CLASS GROUP:_____
SCHOOL:_____

Please read the accompanying paragraph and tick in the corresponding column to what degree each child would match the descriptor:

The child is sometimes disobedient and can, at times, be slow to follow directions. The child may have experienced some problems getting along with others, been observed dominating or bullying others, engaged in temper tantrums and/or responded aggressively to particular situations. The child is sometimes impulsive and can struggle to maintain concentration, stay on task, wait their turn, sit still and/or keep focused.

CHILD'S NAME	Often like this child	Sometimes like this child	Rarely like this child

TEACHER'S SIGNATURE:_____ **DATE:**_____

STAGE TWO SCREENING MEASURE
CONFIRMATION CHECKLIST

Of the list of children identified for inclusion in the study, please indicate whether any of the children:

- speak English as their second language (please list children's names):

- experience problematic anxiety? (please list children's names):

- have evidence of learning problems? (please list children's names):

- present any significant language delays? (please list children's names):

Please complete the following items corresponding to the list of children identified for inclusion in the study:

1) List any child who is **not** aged 4 or 5? (please list children's names):

2) List any child who has any major mental or physical illness including neurological impairment? (please list children's names):

3) According to your understanding list any child who **has** been diagnosed and/or **is** being treated for ADHD? (please list children's names):

4) List any child who has been diagnosed as having ADHD, whose condition is controlled by medical treatment, but who **continues to present problems in the classroom**?

TEACHER'S SIGNATURE:_____ **DATE:**_____

THANK YOU FOR YOUR TIME

Appendix C
Recruitment Letter

Chief Investigators:	Stephen Larmar	07 3311 2314
	Dr Ian Shochet	07 3875 3353
	Professor Mark Dadds	02 9385 3538

Information for Participants

Early Impact: The development and evaluation of an early intervention and prevention program for children and families.

Project Coordinator: Stephen Larmar   Phone: 3311 2314
Project Assistant: Olivia Gatfield Phone: 0422 659320

**School of Applied Psychology,
Faculty of Health Sciences,
Griffith University.**

Junction Park Primary School, together with nine other schools in the Brisbane Metropolitan district, has been selected to be part of a trial developed by Griffith University to introduce the Early Impact program (EI program) into Queensland schools. This program is intended to promote positive behaviours in infant aged children. The trial is part of the project coordinator's PhD research conducted through Griffith University. As you are no doubt aware, managing young children can present a significant challenge to both parents and teachers. The preschool and year one age group have been chosen because of the challenging role that schools and families face in best accommodating the needs of young children.

Junction Park Primary School is working with Griffith University to introduce the Early Impact program to your school's preschool and year one students as part of the school curriculum. This will consist of two half-hour sessions conducted each week over the second term of the school year. In addition, supplementary sessions will be facilitated for the remainder of the school year, consisting of approximately a half-hour session per fortnight. The curriculum explores concepts such as positive communication, friendship formation, social problem solving, developing self-control, and engaging in pro-social behaviours and is designed to promote academic and social success.

We are asking for your consent to allow your child to participate in the project and for you to complete a series of short questionnaires that will enable us to evaluate the success of the program. The questionnaires will be posted to you at the beginning of the program, at the end of the second term and at the end of the school year. In this way we can identify some of the potential positive effects on those children participating in the program. The questionnaires will gather information relating to the child's behaviour and the school and families' interactions with the child. The information contained in all questionnaires will be treated as strictly confidential. We are also asking parents to agree to the school providing us with details regarding children's academic and social progress. Further, each participating child will be invited to answer a short series of questions relating to their class environment.

Parents will also be invited to attend a series of child management training workshops focussing on skills to assist them in effectively managing young children. The workshops will be held on three consecutive evenings towards the end of term one.

If at any time during the course of the project your child requires additional support beyond what we can provide during the program, the Principal of Junction Park Primary School will be advised and will take the appropriate action.

If after reading all the information, you are willing to give your consent to the above, please remove and complete the consent form (attached) and return it to your child's preschool teacher by **Monday February 17th, 2003**. The preschool will forward the forms to the project coordinator. A copy of the consent form will be provided to the school to authorise your child's participation in the project.

Griffith University requires that all participants be informed that if they have any complaints concerning the manner in which the research project is conducted they may be directed to the project coordinator, or, if an independent person is preferred, either:

- the University's research Ethics Officer, Office for Research, Bray Centre, Griffith University, Kessels Road, Nathan, Qld 4111 Phone: (07) 3875 6618 or;
- the Pro Vice-Chancellor (Administration), Bray Centre, Griffith University, Kessels Road, Nathan, Qld 4111 Phone: (07) 3875 7343

If you have any questions or concerns about any aspect of the project now or over the duration of the project please do not hesitate to contact the project coordinator Stephen Larmar on 3311 2314 or the project assistant Olivia Gatfield on 0422 659320. At the conclusion of the project we will forward to you a brief report of the project's findings.

Griffith University gratefully acknowledges your support of its research initiatives. Thank you for your time.

Yours sincerely,

Stephen Larmar
28th January 2003

Project Coordinator: Stephen Larmar   Phone: 3311 2314
Project Assistant: Olivia Gatfield   Phone: 0422 659320
School of Applied Psychology,
Faculty of Health Sciences,
Griffith University.

Thank you for your consent to participate in the Early Impact Trial. Please find attached a series of questionnaires for you to complete. It is very important that as many parents as possible complete the questionnaires. In appreciation for your time we offer the attached complimentary scratch-it ticket as well as your chance to enter the draw to win a family pass to Seaworld and a night's accommodation at the Nara Resort. In addition, the preschool that collects the most parent response forms will win one of two computer packages to the value of $1500. The questionnaires will take approximately 15-20 minutes to complete.
(Please note: To be included in the draw for the Seaworld Nara Resort prize, parents will need to fill out two more questionnaires at later stages in the school year.)
Note: Please return the completed questionnaire to your child's preschool teacher by
_____

Parent/s Full Name/s:_____

Preschool Child's Full Name:_____ Sex: ❑ Male ❑ Female

Age of Child:_____ Child's Date of Birth:___/___/___

Siblings: Your child has how many brothers or sisters? _____

List the people living at home with your child:
Relation (e.g. sister) **Gender** **Age**   **Relation**   **Gender** **Age**

_____ M/F ____   _____ M/F ____
_____ M/F ____   _____ M/F ____
_____ M/F ____   _____ M/F ____
_____ M/F ____   _____ M/F ____
_____ M/F ____   _____ M/F ____

Parent's usual type of work, even if not working now. (please be specific – for example, auto mechanic, school teacher, homemaker, labourer etc.)

Mother's type of work:_____ Father's type of work:_____

What is your current level of education? (please tick)			Your family's income bracket – i.e., income range that both *mother* and *father earned together* in the last 12 months (please tick)
	Mother	**Father**	
No schooling	❑	❑	- no personal income at all ❑
Primary	❑	❑	- up to $5000 (about $100 pw) ❑
Junior Certificate	❑	❑	- $5001 - $12 000 (up to $230 pw) ❑
Secondary	❑	❑	- $12 001 - $20 000 (up to $380 pw) ❑
Current Secondary	❑	❑	- $20 001 - $30 000 (up to $580 pw) ❑
Apprenticeship/			- $30 001 - $40 000 (up to $770 pw) ❑
Trade certificate	❑	❑	- $40 001 - $50 000 (up to $960 pw) ❑
Tertiary (including			- > $50 000 (more than $1 150 pw) ❑
Diploma/Degree)	❑	❑	
Current Tertiary	❑	❑	

Is English the primary language in the home?   ❑ Yes   ❑ No

Strengths and Difficulties Questionnaire

For each item, please mark the box for Not True, Somewhat True, or Certainly True. It would help us if you answered all items as best you can even if you are not absolutely certain or the item seems daft! Please give your answers on the basis of your child's behaviour over the last six months.

Child's Name:_____   Male/Female

Date of Birth:_____

	Not True	Somewhat True	Certainly True
Considerate of other people's feelings			
Restless, overactive, cannot stay still for long			
Often complains of headaches, stomach-aches or sickness			
Shares readily with other children (treats, toys, pencils etc.)			
Often has temper tantrums or hot tempers			
Rather solitary, tends to play alone			
Generally obedient, usually does what adults request			
Many worries, often seems worried			
Helpful if someone is hurt, upset or feeling ill			
Constantly fidgeting or squirming			
Has at least one good friend			
Often fights with other children or bullies them			
Often unhappy, down-hearted or tearful			
Generally liked by other children			
Easily distracted, concentration wanders			
Nervous or clingy in new situations, easily loses confidence			
Kind to younger children			
Often lies or cheats			
Picked on or bullied by other children			
Often volunteers to help others (Parents, teachers, other children)			
Thinks things out before acting			
Steals from home or elsewhere			
Gets on better with adults than with other children			
Many fears, easily scared			
Sees tasks through to the end, good attention span			

Do you have any other comments or concerns?

Please turn over – there are a few more questions on the other side

111

Overall, do you think this child has difficulties in one or more of the following areas: emotions, concentration, behaviour or being able to get on with other people?

No	Yes- minor difficulties	Yes- definite difficulties	Yes- severe difficulties
☐	☐	☐	☐

If you answered "Yes", please answer the following questions about these difficulties:

- How long have these difficulties been present?

Less than a month	1-5 months	6-12 months	Over a year
☐	☐	☐	☐

- Do the difficulties upset or distress the child?

Not at all	Only a little	Quite a lot	A great deal
☐	☐	☐	☐

- Do the difficulties interfere with the child's everyday life in the following areas?

	Not at all	Only a little	Quite a lot	A great deal
HOME LIFE	☐	☐	☐	☐
FRIENDSHIPS	☐	☐	☐	☐
CLASSROOM LEARNING	☐	☐	☐	☐
LEISURE ACTIVITIES	☐	☐	☐	☐

- Do the difficulties put a burden on you or your family as a whole?

Not at all	Only a little	Quite a lot	A great deal
☐	☐	☐	☐

Signature:_____   Date:_____

Than you very much for your help

© Robert Goodman, 1999

112

The University of New Orleans
Alabama Parenting Questionnaire (APQ)
(Parent Form)

Child's Name:_____   ID# (Office use):_____

Parent Completing Form (Circle one):   Mother   Father   Other:_____

Instructions: the following are a number of statements about your family. Please rate each item as to how often it TYPICALLY occurs in your home. The possible answers are Never (1), Almost Never (2), Sometimes (3), Often (4), Always (5). PLEASE ANSWER ALL ITEMS.

	Never	Almost Never	Sometimes	Often	Always
1. You have a friendly talk with your child	1	2	3	4	5
2. You let your child know when he/she is doing a good job with something	1	2	3	4	5
3. You threaten to punish your child & then do not actually punish him/her	1	2	3	4	5
4. You volunteer to help with special activities that your child is involved in (such as sports, girl/boy scouts, church youth groups)	1	2	3	4	5
5. You reward or give something extra to your child for obeying you or behaving well	1	2	3	4	5
6. When at home you are unsure where your child is playing	1	2	3	4	5
7. You play games or do other fun things with your child	1	2	3	4	5
8. Your child talks you out of punishing him/her after he/she has done something wrong	1	2	3	4	5
9. You ask your child about his/her day in school	1	2	3	4	5
10. Your child stays out past the time he/she is supposed to be home	1	2	3	4	5
11. You help your child with his/her learning activities	1	2	3	4	5
12. You feel that getting your child to obey you is more trouble than it's worth	1	2	3	4	5
13. You compliment your child when he/she does something well	1	2	3	4	5
14. You ask your child what his/her plans are for the coming day	1	2	3	4	5
15. You drive your child to a special activity	1	2	3	4	5
16. You praise your child if he/she behaves well	1	2	3	4	5
17. You are unsure of who your child plays with	1	2	3	4	5
18. You hug or kiss your child when he/she has done something well	1	2	3	4	5
19. When at home you are unsure of what your child is doing	1	2	3	4	5
20. You talk to your child about his/her friends	1	2	3	4	5
21. When out of the home (e.g. park, shopping center etc.) you are unsure of where your child is	1	2	3	4	5
22. You let your child out of punishment early (like lift restrictions earlier than you originally said)	1	2	3	4	5
23. Your child helps plan family activities	1	2	3	4	5
24. You get so busy that you forget where your child is and what he/she is doing	1	2	3	4	5

Please turn this page over

25. Your child is not punished when he/she does something wrong	1	2	3	4	5
26. You attend P&C meetings, parent/teacher conferences, or other meetings at your child's school	1	2	3	4	5
27. You tell your child that you like it when he/she helps out around the house	1	2	3	4	5
28. You don't check on your child when they are playing away from you	1	2	3	4	5
29. You don't tell your child where you are going	1	2	3	4	5
30. Your child does not come inside for a long period after you have asked them to do so	1	2	3	4	5
31. The punishment you give your child depends on your mood	1	2	3	4	5
32. Your child is home without adult supervision	1	2	3	4	5
33. You smack your child with your hand when he/she has done something wrong	1	2	3	4	5
34. You ignore your child when he/she is misbehaving	1	2	3	4	5
35. You slap your child when he/she has done something wrong	1	2	3	4	5
36. You take away privileges or money from your child as a punishment	1	2	3	4	5
37. You send your child to his/her room as punishment	1	2	3	4	5
38. You hit your child with a belt, switch or other object when he/she has done something wrong	1	2	3	4	5
39. You yell or scream at your child when he/she has done something wrong	1	2	3	4	5
40. You calmly explain to your child why his/her behaviour was wrong when he/she misbehaves	1	2	3	4	5
41. You use time out (make him/her stand in a corner) as a punishment	1	2	3	4	5
42. You give your child extra chores as punishment	1	2	3	4	5

T 4-16

Strengths and Difficulties Questionnaire

For each item, please mark the box for Not True, Somewhat True, or Certainly True. It would help us if you answered all items as best you can even if you are not absolutely certain or the item seems daft! Please give your answers on the basis of the child's behaviour over the last six months of this school year.

Child's Name:_____   Male/Female

Date of Birth:_____

	Not True	Somewhat True	Certainly True
Considerate of other people's feelings			
Restless, overactive, cannot stay still for long			
Often complains of headaches, stomach-aches or sickness			
Shares readily with other children (treats, toys, pencils etc.)			
Often has temper tantrums or hot tempers			
Rather solitary, tends to play alone			
Generally obedient, usually does what adults request			
Many worries, often seems worried			
Helpful if someone is hurt, upset or feeling ill			
Constantly fidgeting or squirming			
Has at least one good friend			
Often fights with other children or bullies them			
Often unhappy, down-hearted or tearful			
Generally liked by other children			
Easily distracted, concentration wanders			
Nervous or clingy in new situations, easily loses confidence			
Kind to younger children			
Often lies or cheats			
Picked on or bullied by other children			
Often volunteers to help others (Parents, teachers, other children)			
Thinks things out before acting			
Steals from home, school or elsewhere			
Gets on better with adults than with other children			
Many fears, easily scared			
Sees tasks through to the end, good attention span			

Do you have any other comments or concerns?

Please turn over – there are a few more questions on the other side

Overall, do you think this child has difficulties in one or more of the following areas: emotions, concentration, behaviour or being able to get on with other people?

	No	Yes- minor difficulties	Yes- definite difficulties	Yes- severe difficulties
	☐	☐	☐	☐

If you answered "Yes", please answer the following questions about these difficulties:

- How long have these difficulties been present?

	Less than a month	1-5 months	6-12 months	Over a year
	☐	☐	☐	☐

- Do the difficulties upset or distress the child?

	Not at all	Only a little	Quite a lot	A great deal
	☐	☐	☐	☐

- Do the difficulties interfere with the child's everyday life in the following areas?

	Not at all	Only a little	Quite a lot	A great deal
PEER RELATIONSHIPS	☐	☐	☐	☐
CLASSROOM LEARNING	☐	☐	☐	☐

- Do the difficulties put a burden on you or the class as a whole?

	Not at all	Only a little	Quite a lot	A great deal
	☐	☐	☐	☐

Signature:_____   Date:_____

Class Teacher/Form Teacher/Head of Year/Other (please specify)

Than you very much for your help

CLASSROOM OBSERVATION MEASURE

> **CLASS TEACHER:**_____
> **CLASS GROUP:**_____
> **SCHOOL:**_____
> **DATE OF OBSERVATION:**_____

This measure should be completed on each day of the observation week. Please divide the preschool day into three sessions and complete each corresponding section of the measure following each session of the day. The classroom teacher should complete a full observation measure each day (includes the three sessions) and the preschool teacher aide should do the same using a **separate measure**. Ten completed classroom observation measures should have been completed by the end of the observation week. These should be retained for collection by the project coordinator.

Session One:

1)   Please indicate the extent to which one or more children exhibited off task behaviour (please circle):

Very frequently   Frequently   Sometimes   Seldom   Never

2)   Please indicate the extent to which one or more children were disrespectful to you (please circle):

Very frequently   Frequently   Sometimes   Seldom   Never

3)   Please indicate the extent to which one or more children failed to follow directions (please circle):

Very frequently   Frequently   Sometimes   Seldom   Never

4)   Please indicate the extent to which one or more children were physically or verbally aggressive towards another member of the class (please circle):

Very frequently   Frequently   Sometimes   Seldom   Never

5)   Group's Behaviour (please circle):

Excellent   Good   Average   Poor   Very Poor

6)   My confidence in managing the class group (please circle):

Very Confident   Confident   Average Confidence   Little Confidence   No Confidence

Please complete the section over the page...

Session Two:

1) Please indicate the extent to which one or more children exhibited off task behaviour (please circle):

Very frequently   Frequently   Sometimes   Seldom   Never

2) Please indicate the extent to which one or more children were disrespectful to you (please circle):

Very frequently   Frequently   Sometimes   Seldom   Never

3) Please indicate the extent to which one or more children failed to follow directions (please circle):

Very frequently   Frequently   Sometimes   Seldom   Never

4) Please indicate the extent to which one or more children were physically or verbally aggressive towards another member of the class (please circle):

Very frequently   Frequently   Sometimes   Seldom   Never

5) Group's Behaviour (please circle):

Excellent   Good   Average   Poor   Very Poor

6) My confidence in managing the class group (please circle):

Very Confident   Confident   Average Confidence   Little Confidence   No Confidence

Session Three:

1) Please indicate the extent to which one or more children exhibited off task behaviour (please circle):

Very frequently   Frequently   Sometimes   Seldom   Never

2) Please indicate the extent to which one or more children were disrespectful to you (please circle):

Very frequently   Frequently   Sometimes   Seldom   Never

3) Please indicate the extent to which one or more children failed to follow directions (please circle):

Very frequently   Frequently   Sometimes   Seldom   Never

4) Please indicate the extent to which one or more children were physically or verbally aggressive towards another member of the class (please circle):

Very frequently   Frequently   Sometimes   Seldom   Never

5) Group's Behaviour (please circle):

Excellent   Good   Average   Poor   Very Poor

6) My confidence in managing the class group (please circle):

Very Confident   Confident   Average Confidence   Little Confidence   No Confidence

Appendix I

PEER NOMINATION INSTRUMENT

CLASS TEACHER:_____
CLASS GROUP:_____
SCHOOL:_____

Please record the names of up to three children in your class who you think the statement describes:

Descriptor	Name	Name	Name
1) A good leader			
2) Is helpful to others			
3) Is happy at school			
4) Hits and pushes others			
5) Yells and calls others mean names			
6) Starts fights			
7) Is bossy with their friends			
8) Doesn't let other people be their friend			
9) Seems sad at school			
10) Seems lonely at school			

RECORDER'S SIGNATURE:_____ **DATE:**_____

TEACHER SELF-REPORT

> **CLASS TEACHER:**_____
>
> **SCHOOL:**_____

Please complete the following self-report relating to your experiences in implementing the program and retain for collection by the Program Co-ordinator.

Program Implementation:

1) I have applied the strategies of management with the following measure of consistency (please circle):

   100%-80%   79%-60%   59%-40%   39%-20%   19%-0%

2) Throughout the implementation of the Early Impact Program I have endeavoured to include all students with the following measure of consistency (please circle):

   100%-80%   79%-60%   59%-40%   39%-20%   19%-0%

3) I have actively encouraged children to consider pro-social responses as an alternative to inappropriate behavioural choices (please circle):

   100%-80%   79%-60%   59%-40%   39%-20%   19%-0%

4) I have delivered the Early Impact Program curriculum with the following measure of regularity (please circle):

   100%-80%   79%-60%   59%-40%   39%-20%   19%-0%

5) I have adhered to the curriculum delivery guidelines with the following measure of consistency (please circle):

   100%-80%   79%-60%   59%-40%   39%-20%   19%-0%

6) I have encouraged each class member to actively participate in the curriculum component of the Early Impact Program (please circle):

   100%-80%   79%-60%   59%-40%   39%-20%   19%-0%

7) I have endeavoured to maintain regular contact with parents, where necessary, with the following measure of consistency (please circle):

   100%-80%   79%-60%   59%-40%   39%-20%   19%-0%

Please complete the section over the page...

TEACHER SELF-REPORT

Page Two

Perceived levels of stress and confidence:

8) When dealing with the class group my perceived level of stress at this point in the program could be rated according to the following (please circle):

100%-80%   79%-60%   59%-40%   39%-20%   19%-0%

9) In applying the management strategies to the students in my class my level of confidence could be rated according to the following (please circle):

100%-80%   79%-60%   59%-40%   39%-20%   19%-0%

10) In applying the curriculum to the class group my level of confidence could be rated according to the following (please circle):

100%-80%   79%-60%   59%-40%   39%-20%   19%-0%

Classroom Behaviour:

11) The class group are well behaved for what percentage of time? (please circle):

100%-80%   79%-60%   59%-40%   39%-20%   19%-0%

12) My ability to manage the class group could be rated using the following descriptor (please circle):

Excellent   Good   Adequate   Poor   Very Poor

13) Children exhibiting problem behaviours are well behaved for what percentage of time? (please circle):

100%-80%   79%-60%   59%-40%   39%-20%   19%-0%

Program Design:

14) The design of the Early Impact Program has provided a framework to assist me in working more effectively with children exhibiting problem behaviours. (please circle):

Strongly Agree   Agree   Uncertain   Disagree   Strongly Disagree

15) The Early Impact Program has provided further assistance for those children at-risk for the development of problem behaviours. (please circle):

Strongly Agree   Agree   Uncertain   Disagree   Strongly Disagree

THANK YOU FOR YOUR TIME

Dear Parent/Guardian,

To further assist us with our data collection as part of the Early Impact trial we would appreciate you completing the following self-report and returning it to your child's preschool teacher by Friday June 27.

PARENT SELF-REPORT

PARENT'S NAME:_____
CHILD'S NAME:_____

1) When disciplining my child I feel confident using the strategies I have learnt (please circle):

Strongly Agree   Agree   Undecided   Disagree   Strongly Disagree

2) Since attending the Parent Training sessions I feel more confident about disciplining my child (please circle):

Strongly Agree   Agree   Undecided   Disagree   Strongly Disagree

3) I have found the strategies I have learnt have helped me to discipline my child (please circle):

Strongly Agree   Agree   Undecided   Disagree   Strongly Disagree

4) Since attending the parent training my ability to manage my child has improved (please circle):

Strongly Agree   Agree   Undecided   Disagree   Strongly Disagree

5) I have kept in touch with my child's teacher throughout the year (please circle):

Strongly Agree   Agree   Undecided   Disagree   Strongly Disagree

THANK YOU FOR YOUR TIME

BEHAVIOUR CONSULTANT SELF-REPORT

CONSULTANT'S NAME:_____
CHILD'S NAME:_____
SCHOOL:_____

Please complete the following self-report relating to your experiences in working with the referred child and retain for collection by the Program Coordinator.

1) I have met with the child on a weekly basis with the following measure of consistency (please circle):

100%-80%   79%-60%   59%-40%   39%-20%   19%-0%

2) I have employed strategies that closely align with those developed for inclusion in Early Impact to facilitate program consistency (please circle):

100%-80%   79%-60%   59%-40%   39%-20%   19%-0%

3) I have actively encouraged the child to consider pro-social responses as an alternative to inappropriate behavioural choices (please circle):

100%-80%   79%-60%   59%-40%   39%-20%   19%-0%

4) In my meeting with the child I have referred to concepts explored in the program curriculum with the following measure of regularity (please circle):

100%-80%   79%-60%   59%-40%   39%-20%   19%-0%

5) I have made weekly contact with the child's teacher in order to provide additional support for their management of the child and delivery of the program (please circle):

100%-80%   79%-60%   59%-40%   39%-20%   19%-0%

Please complete the section over the page…

123

BEHAVIOUR CONSULTANT SELF-REPORT

Page Two

6) I would rate my confidence in providing additional support to the child during the program according to the following percentile range (please circle):

100%-80%   79%-60%   59%-40%   39%-20%   19%-0%

7) I have endeavoured to keep the child's parent informed regarding key concepts covered with the child in each session with the following measure of consistency (please circle):

100%-80%   79%-60%   59%-40%   39%-20%   19%-0%

THANK YOU FOR YOUR TIME

LaVergne, TN USA
27 March 2011
221636LV00003B/129/P

9 783843 353946